Analyzing & Reporting
Focus Group Results

Richard A. Krueger

Analyzing & Reporting Focus Group Results

Focus Group Kit **6**

SAGE Publications
International Educational and Professional Publisher
Thousand Oaks   London   New Delhi

For information:

SAGE Publications, Inc.
2455 Teller Road
Thousand Oaks, California 91320
E-mail: order@sagepub.com

SAGE Publications Ltd.
6 Bonhill Street
London EC2A 4PU
United Kingdom

SAGE Publications India Pvt. Ltd.
M-32 Market
Greater Kailash I
New Delhi 110 048 India

Printed in the United States of America

Library of Congress Cataloging-in-Publication Data

Morgan, David L., Krueger, Richard A.
 The focus group kit.
   p.   cm.
 Includes bibliographical references and indexes.
 Contents: v. 1. The focus group guidebook/David L. Morgan.   v. 2. Planning focus groups/David L. Morgan.   v. 3. Developing questions for focus groups/Richard A. Krueger. v. 4. Moderating focus groups/Richard A. Krueger.   v. 5. Involving community members in focus groups/Richard A. Krueger, Jean A. King.   v. 6. Analyzing and reporting focus group results/Richard A. Krueger.

ISBN 0-7619-0760-2 (pbk.: The focus group kit: alk. paper)

1. Focus groups. I. Title. II. Series. III. Morgan, David L. IV. Krueger, Richard A.

H61.28K778 1997
001.4'33—dc21   97-21135

ISBN 0-7619-0818-8 (v. 1 pbk.)
ISBN 0-7619-0817-X (v. 2 pbk.)
ISBN 0-7619-0819-6 (v. 3 pbk.)
ISBN 0-7619-0821-8 (v. 4 pbk.)
ISBN 0-7619-0820-X (v. 5 pbk.)
ISBN 0-7619-0816-1 (v. 6 pbk.)

This book is printed on acid-free paper.

99 00 01 02 03 10 9 8 7 6 5 4 3

Acquiring Editor:	Marquita Flemming
Editorial Assistant:	Frances Borghi
Production Editor:	Diana E. Axelsen
Production Assistant:	Karen Wiley
Typesetter/Designer:	Janelle LeMaster
Cover Designer:	Ravi Balasuriya
Cover Illustration:	Anahid Moradkhan
Print Buyer:	Anna Chin

Brief Table
of Contents

Detailed Table of Contents

Acknowledgments

My roots in textual analysis go back to undergraduate studies at Bethel College and to religious leaders who taught Biblical interpretation. Their painstaking rigor taught me that words have a beautiful ability to communicate. These teachers taught me that words were special and that diligence and care were needed to unlock what was meant.

This book builds on a rich legacy of academic researchers who have insisted on careful attention to systematic procedures. These scholars come from many disciplines. Their skill is complex and often undervalued, but they've contributed greatly to our understanding of language and communication.

Mary Anne Casey and I have worked together on a number of focus group projects. She has taught me a great deal about the analysis and reporting process, and much of what is contained in this book grows out of her common sense and insightful approaches. Her solid grounding in academic approaches combined with her practical, no-nonsense writing style have created scores of high-quality and very readable reports.

Michael Q. Patton has taught me how to think about analysis. He has the remarkable ability to get to the heart of the issue and describe it in no-nonsense terms. He continually raised my level of understanding through the careful processing of information. These tools are indispensable to the analyst.

David Morgan, friend and valued colleague, invited me to assist in the preparation of this collection of books and has been invaluable in offering suggestions and strategies that clarify the writing and presentation of ideas.

I'm indebted to a cadre of professional moderators who continually strive to improve their own skills. Day after day they are on the road, listening, analyzing, and presenting results. They are a wonder to watch because they move seamlessly through the analysis process, produce results on time, and do it with the highest of quality. Marilyn Raush and Reyn Kinzey are examples of such people; I am grateful for their additions to this volume.

Thanks to the many masters of focus group interviewing. They have continually pushed for the highest quality results, and they have taught many others by their personal example, their writing, and their sharing of ideas. While many names could be mentioned, I am particularly appreciative to Saul Ben-Zeev, Harold Cook, Mary Debus, Thomas Greenbaum, Naomi Henderson, Judy Langer, Tom Quirk, and Susan Schwartz McDonald.

The production quality was improved by Susan Wladaver-Morgan, who offered editing suggestions. The staff at Sage Publications continually were most helpful. Their editors were encouraging, creative, and willing to take risks. Special thanks to Diana Axelsen, Ravi Balasuriya, Marquita Flemming, and C. Deborah Laughton for eagerly contributing their talents.

A good book is one that touches us in several ways. It should be serious, yet funny. It should be challenging, yet comfortable. It should raise the level of thought. But most of all, it should be fun to read. The best test is if you read more than what you intended. I hope that this book does that for you. May you find the insight, the seriousness, the guiding principles, and the humor in this volume.

Introduction to the Focus Group Kit

We welcome you to this series of books on focus group interviewing. We hope that you find this series helpful. In this section we would like to tell you a bit about our past work with focus groups, the factors that led to the creation of this series, and an overview of how the book is organized.

We began our studies of focus group interviewing about the same time. Our academic backgrounds were different (David in sociology and Richard in program evaluation) and yet we were both drawn to focus group interviewing in the 1980s. We both had books published in 1988 on focus group interviewing that resulted from your research and practice with the methodology. At that time we were unaware of one another's work and were pleased to begin a collegial relationship. Over the years we've continued our studies independently, and occasionally our paths crossed and we had an opportunity to work together. In the last decade, we've worked together in writing articles, sharing advice on research studies, and teaching classes. We have generally found that we shared many common thoughts and concerns about focus group interviewing.

During the 1990s, we found that interest in focus groups continued and we both prepared second editions for our 1988 books. In 1995, the staff at Sage Publications asked us to consider developing a more in-depth treatment of focus group interviewing that would allow for more detail and guide researchers beyond the basic issues. We pondered the request and thought about how the materials might be presented. We weighed a variety of options and finally developed the kit in its present form. We developed this kit in an effort to help guide both novices and experts.

In these books the authors have occasionally chosen to use the word *we*. Although the authors share many common experiences with focus groups, our approaches can and do vary, as we hope is the case with other researchers as well. When you see the word *we* in the books of this series, it typically refers to a judgment decision by the specific author(s) of that particular volume. Much of what the authors have learned about focus groups has been acquired, absorbed and assimilated from the experiences of others. We use *we* in circumstances where one of us personally has experienced a situation that has been verified by another researcher or when a practice or behavior has become standard accepted practice by a body of focus group moderators. The use of *I*, on the other hand, tends to refer to situations and experiences that one of us has witnessed that may not have been verified by other researchers.

In terms of content, we decided on six volumes, each representing a separate theme. The volumes include the following:

- **Volume 1:** *The Focus Group Guidebook*

This volume provides a general introduction to focus group research. The central topics are the appropriate reasons for using focus groups and what you can expect to accomplish with them. This book is intended to help those who are new to focus groups.

- **Volume 2:** *Planning Focus Groups*

This volume covers the wide range of practical tasks that need to get done in the course of a research project using focus groups. A major topic is making the basic decisions about the group's format, such as the size of the groups, their composition, the total number of groups, and so forth.

- **Volume 3:** *Developing Questions for Focus Groups*

This book describes a practical process for identifying powerful themes and then offers an easy-to-understand strategy for translating those themes into questions. This book helps make the process of developing good questions doable by outlining a process and offering lots of examples.

- **Volume 4:** *Moderating Focus Groups*

The book is an overview of critical skills needed by moderators, the various approaches that successful moderators use, and strategies for handling difficult situations. Rookie moderators will find this book to be an invaluable guide and veteran moderators will discover tips and strategies for honing their skills.

- **Volume 5:** *Involving Community Members in Focus Groups*

This book is intended for those who want to teach others to conduct focus group interviews, particularly non-researchers in communities. Volunteers can often gather and present results more effectively than professionals. A critical element is how the volunteers are prepared and the manner in which they work together.

- **Volume 6:** *Analyzing and Reporting Focus Group Results*

Analysis of focus group data is different from analysis of data collected through other qualitative methodologies and this presents new challenges to researchers. This book offers an overview of important principles guiding focus group research and then suggests a systematic and verifiable analysis strategy.

Early on we struggled with how these materials might be presented. In order to help you find your way around the series, we developed several strategies. First, we are providing an expanded table of contents and an overview of topics at the beginning of each chapter. These elements help the reader quickly grasp the overall picture and understand the relationship between specific sections. Second, we've attempted to make the indexes as useful as possible. Volumes 2-6 contain two indexes: an index for that volume and an index to help you find your way around the entire kit of six books. Finally, we are using icons to identify materials of interest. These icons serve several purposes. Some icons help you locate other materials within the series that amplify a particular topic. Other icons expand on a particular point, share a story or tip, or provide background material not included in the text. We like the icons because they have allowed us to expand on certain points without interrupting the flow of the discussion. The icons have also allowed us to incorporate the wisdom of other focus group experts. We hope you find them beneficial. We've also included icons in the book to help you discover points of interest.

The **BACKGROUND** icon identifies the bigger picture and places the current discussion into a broader context.

The **CAUTION** icon highlights an area where you should be careful. These are especially intended to help beginners spot potholes or potential roadblocks.

The **CHECKLIST** icon identifies a list of items that are good to think about; they may or may not be in a sequence.

The **EXAMPLE** icon highlights stories and illustrations of general principles.

The **EXERCISE** icon suggests something you could do to practice and improve your skills, or something you could suggest to others to help them improve their skills.

The **GO TO** icon is a reference to a specific place in this book or one of the other volumes where you will find additional discussion of the topic.

The **KEY POINT** icon identifies the most important things in each section. Readers should pay attention to these when skimming a section for the first time or reviewing it later.

The **TIP** icon highlights a good practice to follow or something that has successfully worked for us.

We hope you find this series helpful and interesting.

—Richard A. Krueger
St. Paul, Minnesota

—David L. Morgan
Portland, Oregon

About This Book

In the early years of focus group interviews, from the late 1950s through the 1960s, focus groups were seldom used by academics. One of the main reasons that focus groups weren't accepted by academics was analysis. Simply put, analysis was confusing, and it was difficult to develop systematic protocol that would apply to the diversity of situations encountered. Focus groups were different in major ways from other interviewing situations. In this book, we hope to identify the distinctive features of focus group analysis and suggest strategies that will improve the quality of analysis.

We're sharing ideas and suggestions as we would offer them to a friend—a friend who is about to analyze focus groups. When sharing with friends, our intent is to accomplish the desired results in a pragmatic manner. We offer strategies that we've found to be helpful in doing analysis.

An assumption inherent in this book is that you probably won't read the volume from beginning to end. While it is certainly feasible to use the book in that way, we've found that many researchers regularly skip sections, go back and forth to topics of interest, and skim other chapters. We've tried to organize the book so that you can quickly find areas of concern and just maybe discover some interesting information along the way that you hadn't anticipated. We will feel successful if you find more than you anticipated in this book.

Part I

The Foundation

Commit yourself to the highest quality of analysis possible with the resources you have available. The analysis is a reflection of your ability as a focus group researcher. Begin analysis with the same level of dedication and seriousness as if *you* were the decision maker or client. If you were making the decision, shaping the policy, or designing the strategy, what would you invest in the effort to make it high quality?

> During World War II, the U.S. government discovered that its parachutes failed to open 5 percent of the time. Clearly, nothing less than zero defects was an acceptable level of quality. How do you tell paratroopers going on a mission that one out of twenty of the parachutes is not going to open? The problem was solved by requiring parachute packers and inspectors to put on one of their products occasionally and jump out of a plane. Parachute quality quickly improved from 95 percent to 100 percent. (LeBoeuf, 1985, p. 75)

Assume you are jumping out into the unknown, and only the results of your analysis will save you. Invest the amount of effort needed to be confident in your results.

In Part I, we will explore the foundation of focus group analysis. This foundation is critical, because it sets the stage for the adapting, revising, and modifying that occur in practice. The principles and approaches contained in the following chapters serve as a baseline to the analyst. The analyst can veer from these principles, but changes should be thoughtful, deliberate, and documented.

1

Introduction to Analysis

Overview

The Concept of Analysis
What Makes Qualitative Analysis Complex?

In qualitative research, we are open to different ways of seeing the world. We make few assumptions about how things work, and we are careful about attributing causation. We strive to be open to the reality of others. We seek to tell someone else's story, but we must listen before we can understand. Analysis begins with careful listening.

We've been told that the scientific method is built on precision, careful formulas, and control over the environment. Yet, in qualitative inquiry, the researcher must begin at a different point with fewer assumptions and an openness to alternatives. This is disquieting for some researchers.

For some, analysis of focus groups comes easily. Others have great difficulty separating their personal views from what is said by participants, they key on trivial points, or they forget that they are seeking the needle and instead give us the haystack. We've seen teens conduct top-quality analysis, and we've seen Ph.D.s struggle and miss the mark. Education helps, but education is not the solution. Openness to new ideas, approaches, and concepts is essential.

Key characteristics of focus group analysis include a disciplined process, systematic steps, a defined protocol, verifiable results, and multiple feedback loops. The analyst must be ready to explain the analysis process. Failure to do so fosters mistrust and doubt.

Consider the Power of a Label

As you seek to describe your analysis strategy, consider calling it by name. Use a label or title to describe your strategy. Labels used in current practice are often preferable to newly coined words. The label by itself can be influential. For example, successful healers have found that it is vitally important that a name be given to identify the disease, ailment, or condition. Without a name, the patient feels a sense of hopelessness and abandonment. The name conveys a sense of classification, of meaning, and, for the patient, a sense of hope. In a similar way, it is important for the qualitative analyst to have a name for the process used. Names are derived from authors, publications, or established concepts such as those described by Tesch (1990) or Patton (1990).

The focus group analyst will never be immune to criticism. When criticism of your analysis comes, be open to it and then strive to learn from this feedback. Indeed, criticism can be helpful.

The Concept of Analysis

Analysis starts by going back to the intent of the study. At times, the purpose of the study is narrow, and elaborate analysis is unneeded and inappropriate. The problem drives analysis. Difficulties emerge in both qualitative and quantitative analysis when there is a mismatch between analytical resources and the problem. This can result in elaborate analysis related to a trivial problem or inadequate analysis of a complex problem of major concern. The researcher must remember the intent of the study and regularly weigh options against two factors: available resources and the value of new information provided by the research.

In some respects, beginning the analysis is like standing at the entrance of a maze. Several different paths are readily apparent at the beginning, and as you continue, additional paths and choices emerge. You don't know if a path will be productive until it has been explored, but the process of exploration requires an investment of effort, even if it is just to peek around the corner.

Survival requires a clear fix on the purpose of the study. Even experts can make mistakes if they are not prepared, caught unaware, or attend to the wrong stimulus. Here's a classic example.

**Respect for Our
Ability to Observe**

At a congress on psychology at Gottingen, during one of the meetings, a man suddenly rushed into the room chased by another with a revolver. After a scuffle in the middle of the room a shot was fired and both men rushed out again about twenty seconds after having entered. Immediately the chairman asked those present to write down an account of what they had seen. Although the observers did not know it at the time, the incident had been previously arranged, rehearsed and photographed. Of the forty reports presented, only one had less than 20 per cent mistakes about the principal facts, 14 had from 20 to 40 percent mistakes, and 25 had more than 40 percent mistakes. The most noteworthy feature was that in over half the accounts, 10 percent or more of the details were pure inventions. This poor record was obtained in spite of favourable circumstances, for the whole incident was short and sufficiently striking to arrest attention, the details were immediately written down by people accustomed to scientific observation.

(George, 1936; quoted in Beveridge; 1957, p. 131)

The story does not argue for the abandonment of observation but, instead, for a respect for our human strengths and weaknesses when engaged in research.

What Makes Qualitative Analysis Complex?

Consider the distinction between analysis of words and analysis of numbers. Analysis of numbers can be seductive, because the researcher gains a sense of accomplishment and confidence by knowing exactly the nature of the results. The results of quantitative inquiry come out the same each time the analysis is replicated—if they don't, it's time to fix the computer. Moreover, this analysis is firmly grounded in well-defined statistical procedures. In quantitative analysis, the respondents select numbers that best represent their position on a measurement scale. The researcher's quest is built on the assumption that the scale and the question are appropriate instruments to measure the phenomenon under investigation. Unfortunately, elaborate statistical procedures cannot compensate for ambiguity in questions or responses.

On surveys, respondents are asked to select a number on a scale that represents their point of view. The number becomes a symbol of reality and the basis of analysis. The researcher may not know if the respondent really understood the question or if the available response choices were appropriate for the individual. In some situations, the respondent might find that the response choices are on target but that they apply in only certain cases. When these problems occur, the reliability of the results is jeopardized. The survey researcher attempts to eliminate these factors by pilot testing the instrument; nevertheless, surveys that reduce reality to numbers have inherent flaws in communication—some more than others. This does not mean that we should abandon statistical analysis but, rather, that we should recognize inherent assumptions and treat all data that measure human experiences with adequate humility.

Focus groups present another face of reality because open-ended questions allow participants to select the manner in which they respond. Furthermore, focus groups encourage interaction among the respondents and allow people to change their opinions after discussion with others.

The complexity of focus group analysis occurs at several levels. When a question is asked, two people may answer using different words, yet have the same meaning. The analyst needs to consider how to compare the different answers. Analysis begins with a comparison of the words. Are the words identical, similar, related, or unrelated? The analyst needs to consider other factors as well. What was the context of the comments? Were the two respondents really talking about the same thing when they answered? Did the discussion evolve so that the second respondent was keying her response to a different example? Also, the researcher must consider the emphasis or intensity of the respondent's comment. Another consideration relates to the internal consistency of the comments. Did respondents change their positions later in the discussion? Still another consideration relates to the specificity of the responses in follow-up probes. Were the respondents able to provide examples or elaborate on the issue when probed? The researcher must take multiple dimensions into consideration when comparing responses.

The analysis process is like detective work. One looks for clues, but in this case, the clues are trends and patterns that reappear among various focus groups. The researcher's task is to prepare a statement about what was found, a statement that emerges from and is supported by available evidence. In preparing the statement, the researcher seeks primarily to identify evidence that repeats and is common to several participants. However, some attention is also placed on the range and diversity of experiences or perceptions. The researcher must identify those opinions, ideas, or feelings that repeat, even though they are expressed in different words and styles. Opinions that are expressed only once are enlightening but should not form the crux of the report.

2

Critical Ingredients of Qualitative Analysis

Overview

It's best to begin by identifying the critical ingredients of qualitative analysis. These principles guide our actions. No part of the focus group interview is as poorly structured as is the analysis aspect. This chapter addresses principles that guide qualitative analysis in general and have particular relevance for focus group research.

Analysis Must Be Systematic

Systematic analysis follows a prescribed, sequential process. The process used may vary from one study to another, but the variations are deliberate and planned, not capricious, arbitrary, or spontaneous. Systematic analysis procedures help ensure that results will be as authentic as possible. This is particularly important for graduate students working on dissertations. Faculty members may encourage the use of computers in analysis as one indication of a systematic process.

As processes become more complex and potentially harmful, we institute systematic protocols to avoid making mistakes or overlooking critical factors. Consider the differences between getting in your car and driving off and the process used by a airplane pilot in preparing for takeoff. Even though the pilot has flown hundreds of times and can remember each step in the takeoff sequence, the takeoff procedures are still followed religiously—in part because of their complexity and in part because one step overlooked can influence the operation of the aircraft. Focus group analysis is also complex and subject to human frailties. The systematic protocol reminds the analyst of upcoming steps, but it also communicates to the user of the study that the analyst has attempted to be thorough.

Several systematic steps have proven beneficial in focus group interviews. One is the sequencing of questions to allow maximum insight. Occasionally, moderators will prematurely launch into the key questions before participants have had the opportunity to collect their thoughts. A more systematic process is to allow participants to become familiar with the topic, giving each individual a chance to recollect personal opinions and listen to opinions of others. This is then followed by key questions relating to the core topic of interest and later followed by final summary questions for each participant.

A second systematic step is the process for capturing and handling data. Typically, focus groups are electronically recorded with additional notes taken by the assistant moderator. Lack of notes or electronic recordings greatly impedes the analyst's ability to reconstruct critical parts of the focus group.

A third systematic step is the coding of data. As the researcher comes across an idea or phenomenon, a label is attached. When the idea or phenomenon reappears, the label is once again attached. In focus groups, this process consists of codes placed in the margin of the transcript; if a computer is used, a section of text is marked and assigned the designated code. Later, the researcher can selectively retrieve and review information pertaining to certain codes, combinations of codes, or related situ-

Different Types of Questions Are Described in Chapter 4 of *Developing Questions for Focus Groups*

ations. This information can then be reassembled differently from the original version. This process, which is called axial coding, allows the researcher to fracture the data and to reassemble them in new ways. For a more complete discussion of coding, see Strauss and Corbin (1990, pp. 61-74, 96-115).

A fourth systematic step is participant verification. This step ensures that the researcher has adequately understood the intent of participants. This step can occur in several ways, such as including an opportunity for all participants to summarize their thoughts and feelings, the chance to respond to the assistant moderator's summary of key points while still in the focus group, or a post-focus group verification of the written report.

A fifth systematic step is the debriefing between moderator and assistant moderator, which occurs immediately after the focus group interview. This debriefing captures the first impressions and highlights, and then contrasts the findings with those from earlier focus groups.

A sixth systematic step is sharing both preliminary and later reports with participants and stakeholders.

Systematic analysis processes force the researcher to examine and challenge his or her assumptions. Assumptions are made throughout the research process, building on past experiences and striving to make the analysis protocol more efficient. Care is needed, however, because even experts make unfounded assumptions.

Analysis Must Be Verifiable

Another researcher should be able to arrive at similar conclusions using available documents and raw data. Humans have a tendency to see or hear selectively only those comments that confirm a particular point of view or a tendency to avoid dealing with information that causes dissonance. Our training, our background, and our experiences influence what we notice and what we attend to. Researchers must continually be careful to avoid the trap of selective perception. Verification in analysis is a critical safeguard.

For analysis to be verifiable, there must be sufficient data to constitute a trail of evidence. The data stream begins with field notes and recordings taken during the focus group, continues with the oral summary (verification) of key points during the focus group, goes into the debriefing with the moderator team immediately following the focus group, and also includes the electronic recording, with the possibility of an interview transcript.

Analysis Requires Time

Focus group analysis begins earlier and usually lasts longer than analysis in quantitative research studies. In numeric analysis, the researcher waits until all data are available. These numbers are then computer coded and statistically analyzed using accepted protocols. By contrast, time spent in the analysis phase of a focus group research project begins with the first group. A distinctive feature of qualitative inquiry is that data gathering and data analysis are simultaneous activities. Often, novice researchers are not prepared for the amount of time needed in focus group analysis. They may miss important linkages because they treat data gathering and analysis as two separate functions.

**Time Demands
Are Overlooked**

There is an iceberg phenomenon with focus group research. The sponsor sees what is above the surface, which is a portion of the planning and recruiting, but mostly the moderating. Typically, the sponsor has little or no sense of the time required to prepare the analysis, yet often this aspect requires the largest time investment.

Analysis Is Jeopardized by Delay

Delay erodes the quality of analysis. This is particularly a problem in focus group research where the overall analysis period may last for weeks or sometimes even months. Delay is a concern for several reasons. While comments may have been captured electronically, there are other types of input that affect analysis quality that cannot be captured by electronic means. The sense of the group, the mood of the discussion, and the eagerness with which the participants talk to each other are not elements that are included in the transcript. Over time, memories of these background factors fade and get confused with other focus groups. As more focus group are conducted, memories of the recent discussions interfere with those of earlier focus groups, and critical information may be lost.

Therefore, several procedures are advised. First, care must be exercised in scheduling the focus groups. Only a limited number should be conducted in one day, and a reasonable amount of time should be allocated between focus groups. The number of focus groups conducted per day will vary with the length of the focus group, the traveling distance between groups, and the skills of the moderator. Two focus groups per day is reasonable, but analytical risks occur when three or four are conducted. Second, the assistant moderator should be charged with taking careful notes. Moderator notes are sketchy at best. On the other hand, the assistant moderator is able to devote full attention to capturing both what is said and the environmental factors that shed additional light on the discussion. Third, immediately after the focus group, the moderator team should conduct a debriefing, and it is best to record this discussion electronically. The moderator and assistant should share their perceptions of critical points and notable quotes that emerged from the focus group. This task serves several purposes. It captures immediate reactions following the focus group and often provides helpful insights into later analysis steps. Furthermore, for a number of moderators, this is like a mental cupboard where memories of the focus group can be placed before going into the next focus group. The moderator should begin each focus group refreshed and unfettered by the comments made in the previous focus group. Committing impressions and thoughts to a tape recorder seems to free the moderator of thoughts of earlier groups that could interfere with later discussion.

Analysis Should Seek to Enlighten

The guiding principle of analysis is to provide enlightenment, to lift the level of understanding to a new plateau. At times, focus groups point out what decision makers or research sponsors don't already know, but in other situations, they confirm earlier suspicions and hunches. The analyst should ponder what new information is provided by the focus group. In interviews of frequent focus group users, a consistent trend emerges. Focus group analysts who raise the level of understanding and awareness about the problem or situation are clearly preferred. Those who create confusion are avoided in future research.

Providing enlightenment is more than just a problem of analysis. The potential for enlightenment has much to do with how the study is framed, who is selected to participate, the ability to provide interpretations instead of just findings, and the nature of the questions, just to name a few of the factors. Nevertheless, the analyst can often make major contributions to this effort. Several strategies have proven helpful in the past. One procedure is to seek answers to these questions:

- What was previously known and then confirmed or challenged by this study?
- What was suspected and then confirmed or challenged by this study?
- What was new that wasn't previously suspected?
- What implications do these results have for the product or service?

Another strategy is to compare and contrast the results with established theory in social science. Other procedures that may assist the analyst are to present results in terms of typologies, continuums, diagrams, or metaphors that depict how focus group participants view the topic of study. Typologies provide classification systems that enable users to identify critical parts of a larger system. These typologies may emerge either from the analyst or from the participants themselves (see Patton, 1990, pp. 393-400). Continuums are similar to typologies but represent phenomena that are expressed in amounts or quantities. Diagrams provide visual, symbolic images that depict relationships, flow, or connections that are critical to understanding. Metaphors also facilitate understanding by comparing the topic under investigation to another, often familiar, object or thing.

EXAMPLE

Metaphors Can Emerge Rather Unpredictably

Several years ago, I was involved in a project that sought to identify the training needs for a group of professionals. About halfway through the study, researchers found that focus group participants were alluding to different levels of skills. Clearly, not all skills were the same in the minds of the participants, and there was a relationship among skills. As researchers were pondering this phenomenon and how to explain it, one of the team members looked out the window (others claim he was daydreaming). It was a cold, winter day with snow on the ground. Perhaps the sight of snow prompted his mind to wander, but an idea emerged. The researcher said, "The training needs are like a snowman." He tore out a piece of paper from his notebook and quickly drew a picture of a snowman. "Look," he said. "The biggest snowball is the base—the foundation. This describes the technical skills that the professionals say are the foundation to being credible and conducting programs. Then the middle ball of snow represents the process skills. These professionals say that they must be able to deliver, to present, and to communicate their technical information. The top ball is the head—the conceptual skills. The professionals need skills to see the big picture, to analyze the environment, to develop strategic plans, and to think about where it is all going." It was a flash of insight, and other researchers concurred that the snowman metaphor did indeed reflect the comments of participants. (That researcher continues to spend a fair amount of time looking out the window. Who knows what new insights might be discovered there?)

Analysis Should Entertain Alternative Explanations

The best analysis occurs in environments where there is a free exchange of ideas and alternative views are sought out and eagerly examined. We have found it helpful to work with team members. Colleagues are encouraged to offer rival explanations and then expose each suggestion to rigorous cross-examination. In some situations, we have sought explanations from focus group participants or from clients. Over time, several explanations are likely to emerge, because they are more robust and capable of providing understanding over a breadth of cases. Focus group data can be assembled in different ways, with each way having potential for new patterns. One way is to examine data from similar focus groups, while another would be to examine comments from similar individuals across different focus groups.

Analysts seek interpretations that explain a sufficient number of the cases. They attempt to find disconfirming evidence. They make efforts to explain the outliers, the unusual cases, or those that have a minority view. It is not an indication of weakness if alternative interpretations emerge or even if *no* interpretations emerge. In some cases, there may be no unifying explanation of participant views, except that the participants express differing views. The absence of patterns can be a meaningful discovery.

I had problems with a bowl of jelly beans. After a few weeks, they'd begin to stick together, and the colors would fade. Before friends arrived, I would have to stir the bowl because nobody would eat them if they stuck together. I suspected that sunlight was the problem. I knew what heat would do to chocolate, and I just assumed that jelly beans would be subject to melting as well. One day when I was home alone, I heard the sound of someone stirring the jelly beans. I knew the sound because I had stirred them myself many times. A glance around the corner caused me to revise my interpretation of causation. My dog, Lindy, a 3-year-old cockapoo, was licking the jelly beans in the bowl. I immediately decided that I needed a cover for the bowl, and then smiled as I thought of all my friends who had been eating jelly beans. Interesting how only a little additional information can drastically change the interpretation!

TIP

New Information Can Change the Way We See a Problem

Analysis Is Improved by Feedback

Analysis benefits from multiple insights and perspectives. Corrective feedback is available from four sources: group participants, co-researchers, experts who were not present in the focus group, and decision makers.

**See Chapter 4
in *Moderating
Focus Groups*
or Chapter 4 in
*Developing
Questions for
Focus Groups***

Focus group participants can provide feedback at several times, but the analyst must seek it out. The most immediate and often the most beneficial feedback occurs at the end of the focus group itself. At the end of the focus group, the moderator or assistant moderator might offer a brief summary of critical points. Participants are invited to amend or change this oral summary, and if suggestions are offered, the group is asked to confirm or correct the new ideas. Providing a succinct 3-minute summary of a 90-minute discussion is daunting but well worth the effort.

Participants can also be invited to provide feedback to draft reports that summarize the focus group in which they participated. This can be accomplished by mailing out the draft summary and then inviting comment by phone or in writing.

In some situations, where it is important for participants to be aware of the total scope of the project, the analyst may choose to send participants the draft summary (or even the full report) for all focus groups. Participants are more limited in their ability to see the larger picture, but, nevertheless, they should be able to see part of their group discussion within the larger report. In the public and nonprofit sectors, there is another advantage of circulating this draft report. While the initial focus group experience typically sparks interest in the topic, the draft summary allows participants to see the situation from multiple vantage points. It allows the analyst or decision makers to further test the viability of recommendations.

Co-researchers are a rich source of feedback. In most cases, the co-researcher is the assistant moderator, but in some situations, there may be others on the research team who are also close to the project. These co-researchers have the advantage of knowing about the purpose and details of the study, and their background in research procedures is advantageous. Feedback from the assistant moderator is particularly beneficial. Listening and observing without the pressure to ask questions or keep the discussion rolling allows the assistant to place complete attention on the conversation. As a result, the assistant moderator has proven to be invaluable in the analysis process.

Another source of feedback is experts who were not present in the focus groups. These could be individuals who are knowledgeable about the audience, the subject under investigation, or qualitative research methodology. These individuals can be beneficial not only in the analysis stage but also as the study is being designed to comment on the questions and the recruitment strategies. For these experts to be helpful, they will need to be familiar with the findings. Due to their expertise, they may identify insights and interpretations that the analyst did not anticipate.

Decision makers or those who commission the study can also be a helpful source of feedback. Indeed, these individuals typically have the most to gain—or to lose—if the study is not on target. In the market research environment, the decision makers can watch from behind the one-way mirror and can communicate with the moderator while the group is in progress. Notes can be passed to the moderator, and the moderator typically takes a break near the conclusion of the group to check signals with the sponsors. In the public and nonprofit environments, the decision makers are helpful in the development of viable recommendations. The moderator will usually have limited background on the history and traditions of the organization, but these insights are of considerable value in interpreting findings and developing reasonable and workable suggestions for future action.

Analysis Is a Process of Comparison

Perhaps the most useful strategy in qualitative analysis is finding patterns, making comparisons, and contrasting one set of data with another. This is the heart of analysis. Renata Tesch described it well:

> The method of comparing and contrasting is used for practically all intellectual tasks during analysis: forming categories, establishing the boundaries of the categories, assigning data segments to categories, summarizing the content of each category, finding negative evidence, etc. The goal is to discern conceptual similarities, to refine the discriminative power of categories, and to discover patterns. (Tesch, 1990, p. 96)

The focus group researcher compares data within a group and also among groups. One of the dangers of single focus groups is the lack of comparison and the inability to discern patterns. Comparison occurs to an extent within a focus group, but it is of more interest to the analyst to make comparisons across focus groups with similar respondents. Then, as different types of participants are interviewed, the analyst seeks to compare results of these newer groups with what has already been established.

The act of comparison has practical implications for planning. In some situations, there is a limited pool of participants available for focus groups. When this occurs, it is often preferable to conduct more groups with fewer participants. As described in other books in this series, the traditional recommendation that focus groups be composed of 10 to 12 participants is of doubtful value. Indeed, not only does this size limit the amount of input from each individual and restrict the flow of ideas, but it is also

More Discussion on the Size of Focus Groups Is Included in *Planning Focus Groups*

difficult to assemble and moderate such large groups. Consequently, there is greater benefit in conducting two groups of six participants instead of one group of twelve. This gives the researcher the power to compare the results of the two groups.

EXAMPLE

Learning to Compare and Classify

Several years ago, an elementary school had an interesting way of teaching classification systems. The teacher would bring out a large box full of keys and dump the keys in the center of the room. The teacher then told students to arrange the keys. The students would ask questions about how they might do it. The teacher said that there could be many ways and that they should think about it and then place the keys in categories. The kids would eagerly get into the task, discussing possibilities, comparing strategies, changing directions several times, and finally coming to agreement about a preferred method. Sometimes they would abandon that method and use something different. It was always an interesting exercise. Some kids would sort the keys by color or metal (brass, iron, and nickel), and others would sort by size (small, medium, large), and still others by the key type (automotive, house, padlock, luggage, etc.). There were no wrong answers, and after a while, some students would ask about the purposes of classification systems. Was it to arrange keys for future use? Was it for an aesthetic display? Eventually, multiple categories would emerge. The exercise was used to teach the process of scientific classification.

Our experience with focus groups is similar. Lots of data are dumped in a file, and you are asked to make sense out of it. Many ways are possible, and there is value in many different approaches. Before you begin, look over all the data and think about the purpose of the classification. Then, when you're ready, get into the data, make comparisons, and develop your categories.

Analysis Is Situationally Responsive

Qualitative research is dynamic and must be situationally responsive. The inductive properties of qualitative research assume that the researcher makes decisions and refines the quest for knowledge en route. Sample size is clarified en route, and questions are adjusted and fine-tuned en route. The analysis protocol should also be responsive to en route signals from the environment.

Situational analysis occurs when the degree of rigor in the analysis is determined by the situation or the problem at hand, as opposed to a preordained and predetermined protocol. In situational analysis, the analyst does not prejudge the type or nature of analysis needed until he or she has had sufficient exposure to data. Early estimates of the time and resources needed should be subject to modification.

3

Analysis Principles of Particular Importance to Focus Group Research

Overview

Focus Group Analysis Is Unique
Let Your Objectives Guide the Analysis
Don't Get Locked Into One Way of Thinking
Questions Are the Raw Material of Analysis
Effective Analysis Goes Beyond Words
Early Analysis Can Move the Study to Higher Levels
Computers Can Help—or Hinder
Analysis Takes Special Skills—and Some People Can't Do It
Analysis Must Have the Appropriate Level of Interpretation
Analysis Must Be Practical (Appropriate for the Situation)

The principles of focus group analysis have roots in many sources, but two deserve special mention: academically oriented social science research and business-oriented marketing research. Academics bring systematic procedures that ensure rigorous analysis. These academic contributions evolved out of analysis of one-to-one interviews, as opposed to the more dynamic interaction that occurs within a focus group interview. Marketing researchers bring respect for practicality, as well as appreciation of results that are understandable and useful to clients. Each source has contributed greatly, and each, by itself, has limits. The challenge is to develop strategies that use the best of each tradition. The following principles guide analysis specifically for focus group interviews.

Focus Group Analysis Is Unique

Focus group analysis uses many qualitative analysis strategies and approaches. We gather data through observations, conversation, and other means, such as registration forms, background materials, or demographic characteristics. There is danger in assuming that the focus group transcript should be analyzed in the same way as the transcript of an individual interview. Focus group analysis combines many different elements of qualitative research and, in addition, adds the complexity of group interaction. Let's consider some of the elements that make focus group analysis unique.

Focus group interviews produce data derived from a group process in a focused manner. As a result, participants influence each other, opinions change, and new insights emerge. Focus group participants learn from each other, and things learned can shape attitudes and opinions. The discussion is evolutionary, building on previous comments and points of view. Who is influenced by whom, and what is the result?

Some people seek to influence others. They are zealous to convert others to their point of view. At times, others are resistant; sometimes, they do change their views, and other times, they decide to avoid conflict and just not comment. This makes analysis difficult, because if you tune in to those seeking to influence others and fail to recognize the intimidation or the presence of other views, the analysis will be incomplete.

Silence does not imply a lack of opinion. Lack of comment on a particular topic may itself have meaning in analysis. Sometimes, what isn't said can be important.

A community was conducting focus groups to identify strategies for preventing teens from using alcohol, drugs, and tobacco. Similar questions were asked in both teen and parent focus groups. One of the first questions was about the big problems facing teens in the community. Interestingly, teens did not mention a concern over gangs, although this was a top concern of parents. By contrast, in parent groups, no mention was made of the effects of divorce on teens, while for teens, this was the major concern. In this case, the silence in one group was noticeably different from how another audience saw the problem. Later in questioning, teens felt that adults overemphasized the gang issue, and parents did not realize the trauma of divorce for teens.

EXAMPLE

What Isn't Said Can Be Important

Let Your Objectives Guide the Analysis

Your analysis is guided by the research plan. Reflect on that plan. Reflect on the objectives of the study. Although no plan is perfect, it does provide you with guidance on themes, areas of comparison, and the overall focus of the analysis. Because of limited resources, all plans are limited. When the plan was developed, the intent was to seek information of a certain type. The number of focus groups, the categories of people selected for the focus group, the locations of participants, or other demographic factors all help guide the analysis process.

A youth-serving agency wanted to know how it could most effectively prepare their professional staff to develop and implement effective programs for at-risk youth. The research plan called for focus groups with four categories of participants. One category was the agency's professional staff, the second category was staff of other agencies and organizations that work with youth, the third category was at-risk youth, and the fourth category was experts from throughout the nation. This research design told the analysts it was important to compare the comments of the target professional staff with what experts and youth had to say. The staff from other agencies provided insight into local cooperation and strategies for collaborative endeavors.

EXAMPLE

Objectives Guide the Planning and Analysis

There is considerable benefit to thinking about analysis before the research plan is finalized. Have you identified and included different categories of participants to facilitate comparison? Are these different groups the ones that are the most important to the study? Do you have sufficient numbers of focus groups in each segment to identify patterns and common characteristics? These questions are best thought about at the beginning of the study.

The research plan guides and focuses the analysis, but it is not carved in stone. The objectives help determine what is examined and what is not. In the process of conducting focus groups, you will acquire enormous amounts of information, and it is easy to get sidetracked or diverted to other interesting topics. Occasionally, these new, emerging topics become more important to the study than what was originally intended. When this occurs, amend your research plan and document the reason for the change.

Don't Get Locked Into One Way of Thinking

Part of the analysis task is to depict reality as understood and experienced by others. The dilemma is that you don't know how to construct that reality until you've begun the process of listening. Strategies that you've anticipated and frameworks that you've developed in advance may all need to be set aside if they do not conform to what you hear.

EXAMPLE

New Ways of Thinking

Farmers were not attending classes sponsored by local technical institutes. The classes had been created after looking over needs assessment surveys of local farmers. Unfortunately, the courses did not attract farmers. It wasn't until the researchers went out to meet with farmers and conducted focus groups that they discovered the problem. In focus groups, farmers told the researchers that the needs assessment surveys did give the right answers, but just the fact that farmers needed information or training didn't mean that they would attend. The educators assumed that need alone would motivate farmers to seek out training. Farmers described another reality that placed these training sessions in a different context. To farmers, training sessions had to be enjoyable, taught by practitioners, include practical information of immediate benefit, and provide an opportunity for farmers to interact with each other. When researchers understood how the classes fit into the farmers' lives, changes were made, and the resulting classes proved to be well attended, enjoyable, and instructive.

Part of the principle of anticipation is being prepared and doing your homework before the focus group. In the time that you have available before the first focus group, attempt to learn as much as you can about the participants and the topic. What has happened before? What information can give you insight into what might be anticipated?

Yet, familiarity is both an asset and a liability. The more you know about the topic and the participants, the more you are able to make comparisons, understand interrelationships, and derive meaning from participant comments. Unfortunately, that same familiarity can also limit your thinking. You may have made assumptions that have been true in the past that aren't true today. You may have made interpretations that were never challenged. You may feel that you already know everything about a particular aspect of the topic because you've heard it before. The danger of not listening is that, this time, what is said may have a slightly different twist or approach that has major implications.

Questions Are the Raw Material of Analysis

Analysis is directly related to the questions asked in the focus group. A problem that regularly occurs with beginning moderators is that they ask questions that are confusing, complex, and virtually impossible to analyze.

Focus group research produces a phenomenal amount of data, so much so that novice analysts are regularly overwhelmed. Each focus group can produce 10 to 15 pages of field notes, combined with a transcript of 30 to 60 single-spaced pages. A critical aspect in surviving the deluge of materials is to focus the analysis. Not all questions deserve analysis at the same level; indeed, some may be "throw-away" questions that are designed to set the stage. The challenge to the researcher is to place primary attention on questions that are at the heart of the study. Certain questions—we've called them the key questions—drive the focus group, because they represent areas of primary concern to the sponsor. These questions are the backbone of the study. Focused analysis conserves resources, but most important, it enables the analyst to concentrate attention on areas of critical concern.

For More Information Read *Developing Questions for Focus Groups*

KEY POINT

Not All Questions Deserve Analysis At the Same Intensity

Effective Analysis Goes Beyond Words

There is a danger in assuming that responses consist only of the words used by participants to answer the questions. It is true that this is a core component of analysis, but effective analysis goes beyond the words. The actions and behaviors of focus group participants may tell you a great deal about your interpretation. The analyst should observe all factors in the communications: body language, gestures, and tones of voice.

For More Information About Body Language See Chapter 7, "Questions Focus Group Analysts Must Face"

EXAMPLE

A Test of Observation

Careful observation is difficult because it is easy to overlook certain important factors. Observation favors preparation, anticipation, and keen observers. Consider this story told by W. I. B. Beveridge in The Art of Scientific Investigation. *(1957, p. 133)*

A Manchester physician, while teaching a ward class of students, took a sample of diabetic urine and dipped a finger in it to taste it. He then asked all the students to repeat his action. This they reluctantly did, making grimaces, but agreeing that it tasted sweet. "I did this," said the physician with a smile, "to teach you the importance of observing detail. If you had watched me carefully you would have noticed that I put my first finger in the urine but licked my second finger!"

Early Analysis Can Move the Study to Higher Levels

Early findings and insights can be incorporated into later focus group interviews for the purpose of confirmation or amplification. Typically, the first focus group yields a considerable amount of new information, and then each additional focus group produces decreasing amounts of new information. This phenomenon provides an advantage in analysis. The analyst can limit time spent on questions where there is saturation (where no new information is presented) and use this time to seek reactions to emerging theories and insights. Some questions may be eliminated altogether. Others can be asked, but the moderator should carefully monitor discussion and briskly move the conversation on to other topics. For example, the moderator could say, "Let me share with you some topics that have emerged from some of our focus groups; tell me your reactions" or "In our earlier groups, we've been hearing about . . . , what do you think about it?" or "We've been hearing some comments about . . . , and we are not sure what to make of them. What do you think?" Care is needed to avoid the bandwagon mentality ("Everybody is telling us . . . ") and to invite participants' insights into the research process ("Help us understand" or "Does this explain how it works?").

For More Information on Numbers of Focus Groups and Saturation, See *Planning Focus Groups*

Computers Can Help—or Hinder

Computers can help us manage vast amounts of data. We are able to categorize, compare, and rearrange information much more quickly and efficiently than before. What was once done with colored markers and scissors on the living room floor can now be done with computers. At the most basic level, the use of word processing software can greatly ease the burden of analysis. Word processing allows the analyst to move text effortlessly from one section to another. In focus group discussions, not all comments are neatly placed in specific sections. Participants answer questions out of sequence, and text must occasionally be moved to the appropriate location. Other times, analysts may wish to move data around, such as placing all responses to a particular question in one location to compare and contrast responses. With the search functions of word processing software, analysts can seek out key phrases or words from the entire text. On a more sophisticated level, analysts can use special software to code and then retrieve information across several focus groups.

Miles, M. B., & Weitzman, E. A. (1994). "Choosing computer programs for qualitative data analysis." Appendix in M. B. Miles & A. M. Huberman, *Qualitative data analysis*. Thousand Oaks, CA: Sage.

Richards, T., & Richards, L. (1994). Using computers in qualitative analysis. In N. Denzin & Y. Lincoln, Eds., *Handbook of qualitative research.* Thousand Oaks, CA: Sage.

Tesch, R. (1990). *Qualitative research: Analysis types and software tools*. New York: Falmer.

Weitzman, E., & Miles, M. B. (1994). *Computer programs for qualitative data analysis.* Thousand Oaks, CA: Sage.

BACKGROUND

For More Discussion of Software Options, These Reference May Be Helpful

---

The benefit of computer analysis is that it fosters a consistent and systematic strategy. In some environments, this is of particular importance, as in studies with complex data or where analysts must carefully document their procedures. The disadvantages are the time needed for computer analysis, which can be considerable, and the danger that the analysis is using only partial data (e.g., the transcript) and may therefore overlook important factors. Computers can also hinder analysis, as in situations when the analyst simply runs out of time because of the lengthy effort needed to learn the system, prepare the transcripts, and code results. Other times, computer analysis can provide mis- leading signals when overemphasis is placed on counting as opposed to other analysis options. Computer analysis demands complete transcripts, preferably with names of respondents in the text. In some situations, knowing who is speaking is of critical importance.

It's interesting to note who is using computer analysis and who isn't. Computer analysis tends to be used more by academics,

Note the Discussion on Computer Analysis by David L. Morgan in Chapter 8

particularly graduate students engaged in dissertation research. It is less often used by people trying to make a living doing focus groups. The learning curve for software and the time needed to analyze tend to favor the longer time schedule of academic research. The elements needed for computer analysis (complete transcripts, computer support staff, instructional classes, coaching advice, etc.) are time-consuming, costly, and more likely to be available within universities than within marketing research firms.

Analysis Takes Special Skills— and Some People Can't Do It

Good analysts are like good athletes. They are born with certain skills or aptitudes that give them an advantage over others, but if those skills are not refined, disciplined, and honed, their talents will not reach full potential. Some analytical attributes are inherited, whereas others can be acquired. Much of analysis seems to relate to the mental makeup of analysts. Are they open to new ideas? Are they able to step outside of their personal experience and express ideas from the vantage point of others? Are they sufficiently secure with their own feelings to allow and even encourage others to offer divergent views? Do they have a first-rate memory? Can they make sense of information without being trapped by detail? Can they stay focused on objectives and recognize what data are relevant and what aren't?

It has been our pleasure to work with hundreds of students who have conducted focus group interviews. Analysis is by far the most difficult task to learn and to teach. Analytic ability doesn't seem to be related to academic degrees, and in some cases, advanced training may produce a rigid, doctrinaire approach that can actually restrict openness to alternative realities. In a recent study, engineers were deemed to be more creative when they began their formal training than when they completed it. We're not arguing for the abandonment of academic training. Academic training emphasizes a disciplined and systematic belief structure, and it establishes a protocol for accepting or rejecting evidence. It offers a host of theoretical constructs that expose the student to multiple worldviews. It is clearly beneficial if the analyst has had exposure to multiple ways of thinking and knowing. Perhaps as important as advanced academic training are broad-based, real-world experiences with people. Superior communications skills, both oral and written, are also essential.

Analysis Must Have the
Appropriate Level of Interpretation

The level of interpretation of data must meet client requirements but also be practical and manageable for the analyst. A helpful way of thinking about this is to consider a continuum of analysis ranging from the mere accumulation of raw data to recommendations for action.

The Analysis Continuum

Raw data —— *Description* —— *Interpretation* —— *Recommendation*

On one side of the continuum is the accumulation and presentation of raw data. We have seen final reports that consist of only raw data. These reports are transcripts, or abridged transcripts, that present the exact statements of focus group participants as they responded to specific topics in the discussion. These statements might be ordered in categories that are of concern to the client. For example, the statements might be ordered according to level of support (from very supportive to not at all supportive) or in categories by participant characteristics (occupational categories, gender, relationship to program, age, etc.). We don't recommend reporting only raw data because most clients don't want raw data. They want data reduction, and this occurs in the next stage.

Next on the continuum is description, which provides summary statements of respondent comments. When using this style, the researcher sets out to provide a brief description of a theme, followed by verbatim quotes that illustrate the theme. While the presentation of raw data usually includes all responses, the descriptive style seeks to simplify the task of the reader by presenting themes and providing a few typical or illuminating quotes.

The decision of which quotes to include sometimes presents a problem. The selection choice should be influenced by the purpose of the study. If the study intends to describe the range and diversity of comments, then examples should be selected with this in mind. Other times, the purpose is to provide insights of typical, common, or usual ways in which participants respond; if so, the researcher should select quotes that are within the mainstream. In either case, the researcher should specify the means of selection.

Interpretation is more complex. The interpretive side of the continuum builds upon the foundation of the descriptive statements and then suggests what the findings mean. While the descriptive process results in a summary, the interpretive process aims at providing understanding. It is important to remember that interpretation is always rooted in the raw data. The interpretations presented are directly linked to raw data evidence in the focus group.

Recommendation goes beyond interpretation, placing greater attention on obtaining multiple perspectives on the meaning of the raw data, as well as various views regarding future courses of action. At this level, consideration is given to the practical consequences of alternative interpretations and of solution strategies. As one moves toward the recommendation side, additional information, such as organizational history and traditions, influences decision making. With raw data, the attention is on the transcript. With description, the attention goes beyond the words to include the fieldnotes and observations of the researchers. At the interpretive level, attention goes to the meaning of what was said and takes into account alternative interpretations. Finally, at the recommendation level, the data stream goes beyond the focus group to include background information about the organization, sponsor, and larger environment.

The researcher must be clear about the level of analysis and interpretation in order to meet the expectations of the sponsor, keep the study on track, ensure the usefulness of the report, and conserve resources.

Analysis Must Be Practical (Appropriate for the Situation)

Focus group analysis, like qualitative research in general, must be appropriate to the situation. For some researchers, analysis is a black hole that sucks up available time and energy, confusing the analyst in the process and jeopardizing quality of results. To illustrate this principle, consider the following analogy.

EXAMPLE

Appropriate Analysis

You are driving down the highway, and the car is running smoothly and quietly. Suddenly, you hear a new noise coming from the engine. You've driven this car for over a year, and this sound is not one you've heard before. What does this noise mean? Is something about to fail? You glance at the instrument panel for clues, but there are no red lights, and the gauges seem normal. Several options flash through your mind. The best you can hope for is that the noise will go away within a moment or so. Perhaps it is just something caught underneath the car that will soon dislodge. The second best option *is that you drive to the nearest service station and talk to your friendly mechanic. The mechanic looks under the hood, turns a screw, and the noise goes away. The mechanic says, "No charge," and you promise to buy gas from that service station forever. Or, the mechanic, after looking under the hood, utters the words "tune up," which, when translated into common people talk, means, "It will cost you $200 to $300 to get rid of this noise." Worst of all is if the mechanic says "overhaul," which means the solution requires several thousand dollars and a week without your car. The point is that at the beginning, when you first hear the noise, you don't know what is needed for the solution. You don't know until a skillful technician diagnoses the situation using past experience and special tools to gain more information about the problem.*

Focus group analysis often operates in a similar manner. At the beginning of the research study you have a hunch about the type of analysis needed, but evidence presented in focus groups can lead you to change your strategy and approach. You may anticipate a time-intensive, transcript-based analysis but find that the results are readily apparent. The opposite could also be true. Analysis can be simple and straightforward if the patterns are clearly identifiable, when minimal differences exist within the group and across groups, or when participants clearly reject differing explanations and uniformly coalesce around common concerns.

The analyst is guided by practicality. Academics don't usually think of practicality first. Instead, they often think more about the strength of the research design, the defensibility of the study, the consistency of analysis, and how to minimize the weaknesses of the study. With a practical mindset, the analyst is open to setting aside early hunches or plans due to modified or emerging situations. Rigid analysis plans can lead to excessive investigation of trivial matters or a superficial assessment of data that truly deserve intensive study.

Studies vary. Some involve risky decisions. Some decisions may be difficult to reverse or change if they are found unworkable. The environment or situation gives us insight about the nature of analysis. The astute focus group analyst stays in tune with that environment and adjusts strategies accordingly. For example, graduate students submitting dissertations involving focus groups tend to assume that the research is to discover and reveal new insights, whereas the examination committee may be more concerned about whether the students demonstrate sound research and analysis protocols.

Some focus group studies are intended to produce a range of ideas so that decisionmakers can understand the variation of thought. Other times, a focus group study might seek to identify the preferred choice from among several options. In examples

KEY POINT

The Challenge Is to Determine the Level of Analysis That Is Appropriate and Practical

like these, the analysis can be straightforward. At other times, we may be seeking insight into complex human behaviors that differ by participant characteristics or trying to understand how a program, policy, or intervention may influence people and what makes it successful. In these cases, the analysis will tend to be more complex and time-consuming. The challenge to the researcher is to determine which level of analysis is appropriate and practical. There are a number of analysis choices. Each consumes resources, and each yields unique benefits. The astute analyst gives this careful thought.

4

Analysis Considerations for Focus Group Research

Some people wonder what to pay attention to and how much weight to give different kinds of information. Indeed, difficulties have occurred when disproportionate attention is placed on certain kinds of information while other forms are overlooked. This section offers suggestions to guide you.

Consider the Words

Think about both the actual words used by participants and the meanings of those words. A variety of words and phrases will be used, and the researcher needs to determine the degree of similarity between responses. Usually, words are used in a similar manner within a group, but the same word might be used quite differently in other groups. It's easy for researchers to assume they know what a word means, but they may be wrong. For example, the phrase *quality service* can have very different meanings to different people. The challenge to the researcher is to concentrate on the meanings as opposed to the words. In a focus group designed to get information to redesign a state agency program, one participant said the effort was "a plot" by administrators. The word *plot* tells a lot about the level of openness and trust perceived in the process.

An analysis strategy for focus groups that uses only words is asking for trouble. Individuals vary in how deliberate or precise they are in choosing their words. Sometimes, people are careful and exact in their language use; other times, a word or phrase will be used inadvertently or accidentally. The challenge is in deciding what degree of attention to place on words alone. When do we minimize the emphasis on words, and when are words the core of our analysis? We suggest that words themselves should command attention, but these words should fit within a larger pattern of communication. The words should be consistent with other factors in the analysis process.

Avoid Excessive Attention to Words

A graduate student was using the mainframe computer to analyze an interview. The computer program required that the student enter the entire transcript of the discussion; then the computer would analyze the conversation based on language structure and word content. The student was surprised when the printout announced that the interviewee was cerebral and the conversation rated highly as an intellectual discussion. In fact, the conversation had been quite routine. Later, after the student checked the computer programming and the transcript, the problem became apparent. The interviewee repeatedly said, "You know," and this phrase was sprinkled throughout the conversation and used to end most answers. The computer coded the word "know" as a sign of knowledge, but, in fact, the interviewee was repeating a trite phrase.

Consider the Context

Participant responses are triggered by a stimulus—a question asked by the moderator or a comment from another participant. The researcher should examine the context by finding the triggering stimulus and then interpret the comment in light of that. For example, when the moderator asks an open-ended question, the first participant begins recounting a specific experience. These comments then provide a stimulus for the next person, who may overlook the original question and instead respond to the first participant's comments. In other situations, the second participant, triggered by the extreme comments of the earlier speaker, deliberately and carefully attempts to provide a degree of balance in the discussion by going to the opposite extreme. If these kinds of comments are taken out of the context in which they occur, they will convey a different meaning. Furthermore, the context can change when the moderator asks a question a second time, using slightly different words.

The context depends not only on the discussion but also on the tone and intensity of the oral comment. The transcript greatly assists the researcher in analysis, but it has an inherent limitation. The tone and inflection of a comment might be interpreted in one way when heard in a group setting and in another way when read in a transcript. For example, suppose several respondents had responded to a question with exactly the same words but with variations in emphasis on certain words.

At times, the moderator can tell about the context by the tone and emphasis used in the words. In a transcript, these tones are not obvious, and the reader may miss the point. For example, suppose someone said, "This was good." The meaning could vary, depending on the emphasis.

Watch Tone and Emphasis

COMMENT	TRANSLATION
"This was GOOD!"	*(It was good.)*
"This was GOOD?"	*(It was supposed to be good but wasn't.)*
"THIS was good!"	*(This one was good, but others were not.)*
"This WAS good."	*(It used to be good, but not anymore.)*

Concern for the context goes beyond the statements and includes the context of the group. What is happening in the larger environment of the participants that might produce certain types of comments? Sometimes, a political, social, environmental, or personal event triggers a reaction that is not typical. Over the years, we've seen these contextual factors repeatedly. It might be anger over closing government offices, frustration at being required to attend a focus group instead of being at a funeral of a colleague, a press release of some event, or a recent scandal.

EXAMPLE

Remember the Context

Remember the experience of our colleague who flew into Kansas City. When he got there, he found that half the men in his evening groups had canceled that afternoon, and those who did show were visibly tense and distracted. The groups were a disaster. Back in his hotel later, he turned on the TV and saw why.

Everyone was talking about the "sting" operation the police had conducted the night before. The cops had sent letters promising $50 for participation in a "research group" to a list of men wanted for skipping alimony or child support payments. After the men had appeared, the doors closed behind them, and they were arrested. Attendance at groups in Kansas City has never been the same since.

—Trevor Collier (1996)

Consider the Internal Consistency

One distinctive feature of focus groups is that participants occasionally change their opinions during the discussion. After listening to other points of view or hearing others explain their logic, some participants may alter or even reverse their views. This phenomenon is rarely seen in other forms of data acquisition, but it does occur with focus groups. Mail-out and telephone surveys typically yield consistent views, as do individual interviews. Some have considered this inconsistency a deficiency of focus group research. But it is only a weakness if we assume that people don't change their opinions in real life—that once we form opinions, they remain constant. Since this is hardly the case, opinion changes seem to indicate that people in the focus group are functioning in a normal, natural manner. The challenge to the researcher is to discover what is influencing the change.

Participants may have been persuaded to change their views after listening to others in the group. The change may have been triggered by new evidence presented by a participant or by different logic that was considered convincing. In some circumstances, participants have been influenced by the forcefulness of another person in the group. The moderator's task is first to identify that a change has taken place, then to determine if the participant agrees that he or she has changed, and, finally, to determine what prompted the change. This is one of the most difficult tasks of moderating and is easier after the focus group as you track the discussion on a transcript. With experience, however, moderators improve their skills in this area and are watchful of opinion changes and shifts during the focus groups.

It is interesting to note that although the rhetoric of participants may change, they may not feel that they have modified their earlier position. This could occur for several reasons. The participants may feel that the supposedly differing views are not really different after all. We have seen some individuals in focus groups hold seemingly opposing opinions and be unconcerned by the discrepancy. A second possible explanation is that the opinions are conditional. Some participants have expressed opposing views, and when asked to explain, they describe circumstances that justify both opinions. If certain factors occur, then they would support one side, but if other factors were present, then their opinion would be different. For example, focus groups with university students were conducted to test a proposed rating system for courses. The proposal called for a consumer guide to teaching faculty with students rating various professors. Students spoke in favor of such guides, but they also said that these guides would not be a factor in their course selection. This seeming inconsistency was resolved when students explained that, although it was nice to get an idea of the instructor's rating, what was most important in their course selection was when the course was scheduled. Courses had to be arranged around student work schedules, and courses were picked not because of the teaching quality but because of the convenience of the schedule.

There is a tendency to assume that frequency, extensiveness, and intensity are synonymous. In fact, these three factors are really quite different. Here's an easy way to remember them:

Frequency	*How often was it said?*
Extensiveness	*How many people said it?*
Intensity	*How strong was the opinion or point of view?*

TIP

The Difference Between Frequency, Extensiveness, and Intensity

Consider the Frequency of Comments

Frequency reveals the number of times something occurs. In focus group analysis, it refers to the number of times a concept or topic surfaces in the discussion. Frequency does not relate to the number of different people making the comment but only to the number of times the comment occurs. Therefore, frequency could be high even if only one person continually brings up a particular topic. In focus groups, this can become an issue when transcripts do not identify the speaker. Ordinarily, the analyst has the comments but not the names of the speakers. The issue raised most frequently is not necessarily the most important, even when it is raised by a large number of people. At times, a comment will be made by only one person in a series of groups, but it is a gem. It might be a new way of thinking about a problem or a fresh idea.

Consider the Extensiveness of Comments

How many different people talked about a particular issue? This is the measure of extensiveness. This indicator can give the reader a sense of the support for a concept within a focus group or across a series of focus groups. It is often used to describe the number (many, most, some, few, etc.) of participants who are favorable or unfavorable toward a topic, issue, or concern. Although the transcript can give a reliable indication of the frequency of comments, it may not be able to identify extensiveness, unless the names of the participants are attached to the comments or the analyst was in the groups and can remember who made which comments.

Consider the Intensity of Comments

Occasionally, participants talk about a topic with a special intensity, passion, or depth of feeling. Sometimes, the participants use words that connote intensity or tell you directly about their strength of feeling. Intensity is communicated by voice volume, speed, and emphasis on certain words. Individuals differ in how they display strength of feeling. Some may talk faster or in an excited voice, whereas others may speak slowly and deliberately. Some may cry and others pound the table. One clue to intensity is a noticeable change in speaking patterns. For example, non-talkers start speaking, slow speakers talk faster, fast talkers speak slowly, quiet speakers talk louder, and so on. The transcript is virtually worthless when it comes to detecting intensity.

You might be wondering just where to place attention in analysis. On frequency? On extensiveness? On intensity? We suggest that all three factors have a role to play in analysis. The analyst should not be swayed by just one factor or misinterpret one for another. Frequency, extensiveness, and intensity are three separate gauges on your instrument panel, and your task in analysis is to share what each gauge means for overall understanding.

Deciding Where to Place Emphasis

Consider the Specificity of Responses

Responses that are specific and based on experiences should be given more weight than responses that are vague and impersonal. To what degree can the respondent provide details when asked a follow-up probe? Greater attention is often placed on responses that are in the first person, as opposed to hypothetical, third-person answers. For example, compare the following two responses: "Last Saturday my daughter and I went to the Lake Street office. The office person gave us all the forms and helped us fill them out. You know, she really took time to help us. When the phone rang, she put the callers on hold so she could finish helping us. I felt she was really concerned about us. You couldn't ask for better service." The second response is, "The services are good and people in the area should use them." The first carries more weight than the second.

Consider What Was Not Said

This consideration is often overlooked and can be tricky to analyze. What does it mean when something was not said, especially when the researchers have anticipated that a need, issue, or concern would surface? Ordinarily, it means that the topic not mentioned is less important than thought because it did not come to mind or at least was not cited by a participant. This interpretation, however, is risky, because you just don't know the meaning unless you ask. The moderator can handle this in several ways. One is a follow-up question about the missing item. The moderator or assistant might also mention it in the oral summary at the end of the focus group: "The topic of . . . was not mentioned in the discussion, and I am assuming that it's not as important as the other topics you talked about. Is that correct?" You need to catch these things during the group. For example, let's say you don't recognize that the cost of a service hasn't been discussed until after all your groups are done. You don't know if it isn't important or if it just didn't occur to the group. Because of this phenomenon of potentially important topics not being discussed, the astute moderator will seek to analyze each focus group before conducting the next. This allows the moderator to watch for the topic in the subsequent focus group and probe further. Even if the topic is not mentioned in the second group, the moderator might inquire about its importance.

Find the Big Ideas

The researcher can get so close to a multitude of comments and details that trends or ideas that cut across the entire discussion are missed. One of the traps of analysis is not seeing big ideas. It can be helpful to take a few steps back from the discussions by allowing an extra day for big ideas to percolate. For example, after finishing the analysis, the researcher might set the report aside for a brief period and then jot down three or four of the most important findings. Assistant moderators or others skilled in qualitative analysis might review the process and verify the big ideas. At times, the researcher might find an unanticipated big idea that provides insight into how the consumer views the product or service. Big ideas emerge from an accumulation of evidence—words used, body language, intensity of comments—rather than from isolated comments. Look for big ideas not only in the responses to key questions but throughout the discussion.

For example, a university department recently conducted a series of focus groups to determine how it was seen by different audiences, to identify needs within and outside the university, and to suggest future directions. Focus groups were conducted with department employees, university employees not in the department, and residents of the state. An unanticipated big idea emerged after listening to all of the focus groups. There was a marked and distinct difference between how internal department employees talked about themselves compared with how they were viewed by outsiders. There was a feeling among department employees that they were not respected, appreciated, or valued by others, but outsiders were consistently very appreciative and regarded their work highly. In the report, the analyst described a morale problem in how employees felt they were treated. This became one of the major findings, even though the question was not asked directly in the focus groups.

Part II

Doing Analysis

In Part II, we will explore strategies for actually doing analysis. We discussed basic principles in Part I. Now we want to share some field skills that may help you in doing analysis. This includes a suggested process that can guide you in analysis. Also included is a review of tools and equipment that the analyst may find helpful, questions we've often encountered about analysis, and analysis strategies used by several experts. Finally, we conclude with several bits of advice to novice analysts.

5

The Analysis Process

In this chapter, we present analysis as a fluid process rather than as a series of isolated tasks. The process may not flow in the sequence listed. Some steps may occur simultaneously, and sometimes, you'll need to loop back and repeat an earlier step. This sequence is meant to help the analyst think through the entire analysis process, rather than seeing it as something that happens after the groups are done.

At the Beginning . . .
Consider Analysis When Designing the Study

Analysis should be considered when you first begin thinking about the study. From the very beginning, the analyst is moving through several mental time zones (present and future) and giving thought to options, trade-offs, and choices that affect the quality of the study. For example, here are some questions that the analyst might consider early on:

What is the magnitude of the decision? (e.g. changing a newsletter versus building a new church)

How reversible is the decision?

What's needed for sponsors or users to find the study credible and believable?

Will there be corroborating studies or evidence?

What amount of resources are available?

How many groups will be conducted?

Will the analyst be present in the groups?

Will the sponsor be present in the groups?

Do you want to involve volunteers in conducting the groups?

Has the analyst had experience with this particular topic?

What is needed for the analyst to come "up to speed" on the topic?

Will recommendations, suggestions, or implications be needed?

Do you want to publish the findings in an academic journal?

The answers to these questions will influence the manner of capturing and handling the data, the rigor and speed with which the analysis is performed, and the reporting of results.

The researcher will need to reflect on the scope of the study and the sponsor's needs for rigorous analysis, speedy results, and credible reports. These decisions are best made as the study is initially planned, but too often at the planning stage, the concern is on the immediate tasks such as identifying the participants, locations, questions, and logistics.

In the nonprofit and public sectors, the number of options open at the design stage is greater than in private sector market research. Will the study make use of volunteer moderators? Will volunteers be used in other capacities, such as design consultation, question development, recruitment, or development of interpretations or recommendations? In academic research, the analyst will need to consider the credibility of the focus group methodology, particularly in disciplines with rich histories of quantitative research. Other concerns involve the expectations imposed by academic reviewers or the need to document neutral, unbiased methods.

For More Information About Planning the Focus Group See *Planning Focus Groups*

At the Beginning . . .
Discuss Options for Analysis and Reporting With Sponsor

The researcher should discuss with the sponsor options related to the intensity and depth of the analysis and the nature of the reporting. Unfortunately, this step is sometimes overlooked, and consequently, misunderstandings develop between the researcher and the sponsor. Without a doubt, this is a difficult step and one that must be made with incomplete information. Nevertheless, the study must be bounded and limited because resources are always limited. Later, the study can be amended to accommodate subsequent developments.

In some studies, options are outlined in a bidding step, in which the researcher proposes a specific budget and time line for a particular project. However, these options are sometimes not discussed, or assumptions are made by both researcher and sponsor that are markedly different. Our advice is to be as clear and complete as possible with the sponsor, but avoid the impression that you are dwelling on trivia. Occasionally, the client will specify certain requirements for a focus group study and the researcher will respond by offering alternatives.

Factors that can influence the options are the purpose of the study, the resources available, the investment needed in analysis, and the degree of rigor needed. For example, if the study is to be used to make decisions that are difficult or expensive to reverse, like building a new church, then an intensive process is warranted. The researchers will need to estimate the resource investment needed for analysis and offer a recommended analysis strategy, plus other possible strategies that involve varying amounts of resources.

For More About Reporting See Part III of this Volume, "Sharing Results"

At the Beginning . . .
Consider Analysis Implications of Questions

Some questions are more difficult to analyze. They demand more time and perhaps even a careful review of the transcript. These are typically the questions that deal with abstractions or in which language can have multiple meanings. Here the analyst needs to make calculated trade-offs. Certain steps can simplify the analysis process, but doing so may sacrifice the richness of other aspects of the study. For example, the researcher may suggest that the participants place their attention on a predetermined set of topics or request that the participant feedback be provided in predetermined response categories. Suppose a public organization wishes to perform a needs assessment in order to offer services that best meet local needs. The needs assessment can be narrowed in several ways. One strategy is to restrict questions about needs to only those that the agency has been chartered to address, like health, education, or safety. Another strategy is to provide specific cues to generate ideas in targeted areas (health, housing, spirituality, education, recreation, etc.) and then to evaluate the suggestions by rating them on criteria such as importance, practicality, centrality to mission, and so on.

Don't assume that there is only one way to ask questions. Some questioning strategies take more time than others, often while providing more sensitivity and understanding. Other questions may limit categories of investigation in order to provide more discussion of certain topics of interest to the sponsor. Questions that ask participants to design, debate, role-play, project, or discuss will eat up precious minutes of time, and the decision is whether this is time well spent. For example, suppose that you wanted to find out which factors are most important in a study of customer service. Do you want to have a rating sheet with predetermined categories, an open-ended discussion of what constitutes satisfaction, examples of satisfaction followed by the discovery of principles embedded in the examples, or other choices? Some strategies will be easier to analyze or may even involve the participants in analysis, such as in group sharing of observations and then discussion of what is deemed of greatest importance. Questions that are typically more difficult and time-consuming to analyze include creative or projective questions, conceptual mapping exercises, and scales that are determined by the participants.

Questions Are Described in Greater Detail in *Developing Questions for Focus Groups*

At the Beginning . . .
Make Preliminary
Decisions on Analysis Strategy

In terms of the investment of researcher time, analysis is one of the most variable aspects of the focus group process. An early estimate of time and resources is advisable, and those who pay for the study must be involved in the decision. The decision on reporting and the decision on analysis often go hand in hand. The options for analysis are many, and each veteran researcher has favorites. One way to consider these choices is to place them on a continuum of time investment (and rigor). The choices include the following:

Additional Information on Reporting Is Included in Part III of This Volume, "Sharing Results"

← *More time intensive*   *Less time intensive* →

← *More rigorous*   *Less rigorous* →

Transcript-based———Tape-based———Note-based———Memory-based

Usually, you will want to decide on the most rigorous method that resources allow and then scale back if that degree of rigor is not needed.

Option 1: Transcript-Based Analysis

Transcript-based analysis is usually the most rigorous and time-intensive of the choices. Tapes are transcribed, and the analyst uses the transcription, along with field notes and the discussion from the debriefing. For a series of three focus groups, a veteran researcher might allocate 30 to 48 hours for transcript preparation plus another 30 to 48 hours for the analysis process, including preparation of the first draft of the report.

Option 2: Tape-Based Analysis

Tape-based analysis involves careful listening to the tape and the preparation of an abridged transcript. This abridged transcript is considerably shorter than the typical page focus group transcript, which is often between 30 and 60 pages. This transcript contains comments that directly relate to the topic at hand plus the moderator's (or assistant moderator's) oral summary at the conclusion of the focus group. As a result, the abridged transcript may be between 3 and 15 pages long. For the series of three focus groups, the veteran researcher might allocate 12 to 24 hours, including the preparation of the first draft of the report. This estimate assumes that the analysis is conducted by the same individual who moderates the focus groups.

Option 3: Note-Based Analysis

Note-based analysis relies primarily on field notes, debriefing sessions, and summary comments made at the conclusion of the focus group. The focus group is taped, but the tape is used primarily to verify specific quotes and to transcribe the oral summary at the conclusion of the focus group. The primary analysis documents are the detailed field notes. Other information sources provide amplifying details. If more rigorous analysis is later needed, the tapes are available for transcription. Again, for the same series of three focus groups, the analyst might allocate 8 to 12 hours, which includes preparation of the first draft report.

Option 4: Memory-Based Analysis

As one might expect, memory-based analysis relies primarily on memory as opposed to electronic recording. In this analysis process, the moderator presents an oral report to the clients immediately following each focus group. Field notes might be consulted, but much is derived by recall. This analysis strategy is often used in market research environments, where the clients have been watching the focus group from behind the one-way mirror. Clearly, the quality of this analysis process depends on the skills, experience, and memory of the analyst. Novice moderators should be discouraged from using this protocol until after they have mastered the more rigorous strategies. Memory-based analysis is rapid, and, when prepared by a veteran moderator, the results can be impressive.

During the Group . . .
Conduct and Analyze Several Focus Groups

Analysis begins during the first focus group. Now it is time to get into the field, conduct focus groups, and begin the analysis process. Several focus groups may be needed to gain a sense of how the questions are working. Do the questions get people to talk? Are participants talking about the topic, or are they distracted easily or off-topic? Is the information produced relevant to the study? Do questions need to be revised? After a few groups, the researcher is better able to make the decision on which analysis strategy to use.

There are several things you should do before you and the participants leave the focus group. Once participants leave the focus group it is difficult, if not impossible, to tie together missing pieces of the analysis puzzle. Certain analysis functions must be performed while participants are still gathered together.

Listen for inconsistent comments and probe for understanding

Participants in focus groups may change their positions after interacting with others. This topic of internal consistency is one of the analysis considerations that was discussed in Chapter 4. When there is a shift in opinion, the researcher typically traces the flow of the conversation for clues that might explain the change. The shift is noted and may take on importance in the final report if the opinion shifts are relevant to the purpose of the study.

The challenge to the moderator is to identify these inconsistencies while the participants are still in the focus group. This permits the moderator to inquire about the differing points of view: "Earlier you said . . . and now you've indicated that. . . . These seem to me to be different from each other. Help me understand how you feel about this issue."

Listen for vague or cryptic comments and probe for understanding

Sometimes, participant comments seem logical at the moment they are said, but later, with critical thinking, the logic crumbles. This is particularly true with words or concepts that can have a broad range of meanings and that have become well accepted into the vocabulary of participants. Certain words or phrases may seem obvious to some, but if they are central to the study, they deserve amplification. Here are some comments we've heard over the years: "We need diversity!" "Customers must be satisfied!" "We want quality products!" "Pay attention to our needs!"

When you hear comments like this, try using a probe to find out more, such as "Tell me more," "Could you give me an example?" or "Please explain, I'm not sure I know what you mean." Some moderators can get participants to say more by maintaining eye contact, as if they are expecting the individual to keep talking. Sometimes you might try, "Say it again, but use different words."

Clarify Vague Concepts

Several years ago, I was analyzing a series of focus groups that examined the outreach efforts of a land-grant university. One of the questions was on getting people to attend events and meetings offered by the university. Participants said that promotion was essential. A pattern emerged that additional promotion would result in increased attendance. The comments were accepted at face value, and it wasn't until after the focus groups were completed that a skeptic on the research team challenged these comments. She said, "What do they mean by promotion? Is it commercials, personal invitations, newspaper articles, or something else? They're giving you the easy answer. It is easy in our society today to claim that promotion or lack of promotion influences people. But is that the real reason? In areas where promotion had increased, the attendance hadn't changed. If it is promotion, it doesn't operate in a linear way that is directly correlated to attendance." In looking back, we realized we should have been less willing to accept the easy answer. We should have asked for an example or probed for more understanding. It could be that people were talking about a special type of promotion, offered through a particular medium or delivered in a unique manner. Whatever it was, we missed the opportunity because we too quickly assumed we knew what they meant.

For More Information on Capturing Information, See Chapter 11 of *Moderating Focus Groups*

Take careful notes of the focus groups

One of the benefits of assistant moderators is that they can devote their primary attention to taking field notes and capturing important aspects of the discussion. The field notes can include the key points in the discussion, notable quotes, and important observations (silent agreement, obvious body language, indications of group mood, ironic or contradictory statements). This information can provide valuable insight into the nature of the discussion and may not be captured on electronic recording devices. Also, these notes may save the day if the recorder goes on the fritz.

For More Information About Ending Questions, See Chapter 4 of *Developing Questions for Focus Groups*

Consider a final preference question or brief personal summary

In Volume 3 of this series, *Developing Questions for Focus Groups,* we discuss a type of ending question called the "all-things-considered question." This question has proven helpful in nailing down the final positions of participants, especially when they have talked on both sides of an issue or seem to have modified their positions.

Offer a summary of key questions and seek confirmation

This is the first opportunity for the moderator (or assistant) to offer an oral summary of the critical questions. This summary has two advantages. It occurs close in time to when comments were actually made and, therefore, is least subject to memory fade. More important, however, is that this process allows and encourages the participants to verify that the summary is accurate and complete. When giving the oral summary, keep it short (2 to 3 minutes) and limit yourself to the most important points based on the objectives of the study.

Draw a diagram of the seating arrangement

While participants are still in the focus group, the assistant moderator should sketch a seating diagram for the group. Some moderators have found this helpful in recalling the names of participants. A week or two after the focus group, you may not recall the names but you might remember where the person was seated at the table. With the seating diagram, you can attach a name to the memory. This diagram can be valuable as a reference and memory jog if later you should decide to prepare complete transcripts with names of speakers.

Obtain needed background information from participants

Before participants leave the focus group, be sure that you have all the necessary background information. This information might be obtained by one or both of the following methods. First, note and record observable characteristics such as gender, age, race, and so forth. Second, ask participants to complete a registration form containing biographical data prior to the focus group *if* these data are needed. Information relating to status or influence is dangerous to ask in the focus group because of the tendency of such responses to influence other participants. Therefore, information such as income, educational level, size or scope of business, degrees, or employment positions is often better obtained in writing prior to the focus group. An example and discussion of registration forms is included in Chapter 4 of *Moderating Focus Groups.*

Tips on How to Give the Oral Summary Are Included in Chapter 4 of *Developing Questions for Focus Groups*

On Registration Forms, Ask Only for Information That Is Truly Needed

A Little Later . . .
Immediately After the Group

As soon as the focus group is concluded, the moderator team should take steps to ensure the integrity of the data. One task, which sometimes is not easy, is to get participants to leave. In some cases, participants have enjoyed each others' company and clearly are not interested in departing. Once participants are gone, the moderator team should use the next 30 minutes in a productive manner. This includes completing the following tasks:

Spot-check the tape recording to ensure proper operation

The researchers can quickly gain a sense of the quality of the audio recording by rewinding and playing the tape at different points. If problems are apparent, the researchers should immediately reconstruct the discussion using field notes.

**Quickly Checking
Your Tape Recording**

As soon as the focus group is completed, check your tape recorder to see if it captured the discussion. You don't need to listen to the entire tape. Just rewind it to a few spots, push the "play" button, and listen. Rewind about 5 to 10 seconds and also about 60 seconds or so. Listen for both volume level and clarity of voices. If the sound is OK at these spot checks, then you can safely assume that the tape recording is adequate.

Conduct moderator and assistant moderator debriefing

Typically, researchers want to discuss the focus group, and this discussion can be most productive if it is electronically recorded for use in subsequent analysis. First impressions are easily forgotten, and the researcher can lose sight of these initial reactions unless they are documented. In the debriefing, the moderator team might discuss the following:

- What are the most important themes or ideas discussed?
- How did these differ from what we expected?
- How did these differ from what occurred in earlier focus groups?
- What points need to be included in the report?
- What quotes should be remembered and possibly included in the report?
- Were there any unexpected or unanticipated findings?
- Should we do anything differently for the next focus group?

Label and file all field notes, tapes, and other materials

A considerable amount of data is collected in a series of focus groups. Unlabeled field notes or misplaced tapes can cause enormous frustration. Time spent on these housekeeping tasks before leaving the site can minimize frustrations later.

A Little Later . . .
Periodically Review Analysis
Strategy and Adjust as Needed

Changing the degree of rigor of the analysis may not be as difficult as it sounds if the researcher has laid the foundation with systematic data collection methods. Careful field notes and electronic recordings can be used in a variety of ways. Initially, the researcher might plan to prepare a detailed analysis based on transcripts and a careful review of field notes. After conducting several focus groups, it may become apparent from the range of comments that the participants clearly and unambiguously articulate a narrow range of views, and, as a result, detailed transcripts are not needed. In other situations, you may find that you have to increase the level of rigor in your analysis. In a recent study of satisfaction with a health-care system, we planned to do detailed analysis of patient groups and intended to use family member groups only as supportive data. However, after conducting the groups, it became clear that the family member groups deserved equal analysis and reporting.

A Little Later . . .
Conduct Additional Focus Groups
and Possibly Modify Questions

Later, after *some* of the focus groups, the researcher may want to modify the questions or timing, or seek confirmation of emerging themes or ideas. Although most focus group studies consist of three to six groups, some will involve a dozen or more focus groups; indeed, some have consisted of more than 50 focus groups on the same topic. In these studies, the researcher has a special opportunity not present when only a handful of groups are conducted. After a reasonable number of groups, several trends are likely to appear, and occasionally the researcher will identify "big ideas" that were discovered but not sought. When this occurs, the researcher might reduce the time for some predetermined questions and perhaps even eliminate other questions that are deemed unproductive, confusing, or redundant. This allows the addition of new questions that have emerged from earlier focus groups. Sometimes, the researcher seeks confirmation of earlier discovered findings or tests out categories, typologies, or diagrams that were developed from previous groups. For example, you may have saturated a particular concept and find after a number of groups that no new ideas are emerging. At this point, you may want to consider dropping the saturated question and substituting another question that furthers the learning.

At the End . . .
Use Analysis Strategy on Remaining Groups

Once the analysis strategy has been identified, the researcher consistently applies the protocol to additional cases.

At the End . . .
Prepare and Present Report

Analysis and reporting are closely intertwined. The purpose of analysis is to develop understanding out of complexity. The final step is the preparation and presentation of the report.

6

Tools and Equipment for Making Analysis Easier

Overview

Quality Microphone
Tape Recorder
Video Camera
Transcription Machine or Variable-Speed Tape Player
Flip Charts and Response Forms
Computer
Long Table, Scissors, and Colored Marking Pens

The analyst faces the challenge of data reduction. The amount of data collected in focus group discussions is considerable. For example, a transcript from one focus group can easily consist of 30 to 60 single-spaced pages. In a series of four focus groups, the researcher may be confronted with more than 200 pages of single-spaced transcripts, 8 hours of tape recordings, and field notes from four discussions. The complexity of analyzing this mass of data can be overwhelming. The ideal solution would be for the analyst to have an excellent memory, capable of storing all details and retrieving correct data just when needed. Unfortunately, due to limited memories, researchers must rely on other strategies, including using tools and equipment to make the task easier. Some of these have been discussed in other books in this kit, and here we will summarize the key elements.

Quality Microphone

The microphone is perhaps the most important piece of equipment. When conducting focus groups in places like community rooms and restaurants, the acoustics are typically poor. Background sounds are an ever-present nuisance. A high-quality, remote microphone in the center of the table is essential. Note the discussion on the pressure zone microphone (PZM) in Chapter 11 of *Moderating Focus Groups*.

Tape Recorder

As discussed in Chapter 3 of *Moderating Focus Groups,* our preference has been a midpriced, easy-to-operate cassette recorder with a minimum of jacks and buttons. User-friendly simplicity is essential. Our experience has been that the microphone affects the quality of the sound much more than the tape recorder.

Video Camera

The technical quality of video cameras has improved greatly in the last decade. Size has decreased, and image clarity is superb. While the price of equipment has decreased, the professional-quality video cameras in market research focus group rooms are beyond the reach of many nonprofit organizations. A continuing concern is that the video camera becomes obtrusive, changes the environment, and affects participant spontaneity. The benefit of the video camera is the possibility of observing the array of participant actions and basing analysis on more than just words. The decision to videotape the group should be based on the potential influence of video recording on participants, the costs of recording, and the added value that video brings to the analysis.

Here are some creative ways that video recording can be of help. Consider using a video camera to do the following:

- Improve moderator skills. Beginning moderators can practice their introduction to the focus group or even videotape themselves while conducting a focus group.
- Capture the conclusion of the focus group. Consider using a video camera at the end of the group to capture final statements, summary comments, or critical points that have been discussed earlier by participants.
- Videotape the last groups in a series. Once you've achieved theoretical saturation, the video might be introduced into final groups. By this time, the video recording equipment will not affect the analysis outcome, but it will enable the researchers to watch for and capture on video key themes that have surfaced in the study.

For a Discussion of Theoretical Saturation, See *The Discovery of Grounded Theory*, by Glaser and Strauss

Transcription Machine or Variable-Speed Tape Player

Transcription machines are invaluable. These systems allow the transcriber to adjust the speed and tone of the tape recording in order to enter comments with minimal stopping of tape. When the tape has to be stopped, the transcriber presses a foot pedal that backs up the tape several seconds to replay missing information. In addition, these systems usually have both a speaker and headphones for listening. These systems save time and agony in the preparation of transcripts, but they are also helpful to analysts in capturing key ideas, picking out notable quotes, and preparing summary comments.

Variable-speed tape players save valuable time. Some tape recorders enable the researcher to play back the tape at different speeds. The recorder can be speeded up to almost twice the normal speed with minimal distortion or slowed down to about 75% of normal speed to capture the exact words of a critical participant comment. The variable-speed tape recorder costs a bit more than the standard cassette recorder but is well worth the extra investment.

Cassette players with double decks are helpful in dubbing sections of one tape onto another. Reasonably priced double-deck cassette players enable the researcher to listen to a tape and then make a copy of selected relevant comments on the second tape. If needed, all responses to a particular question can be packed in one section of the second tape. This process enables the researcher to play all responses to one question without changing cassettes. Another strategy is to use double-deck recorders to capture a collection of the most insightful quotes from participants. This second tape with selected quotes can prove helpful in oral reports or can be given to key decision makers for drive-time listening. Double-deck recorders are also helpful in making a backup copy of tapes.

Verify the Transcripts

Never completely trust the transcript. If someone is preparing the transcript for you, be sure to verify that the comments as transcribed are exactly the same as those that were spoken. With the best of intentions, some transcriptionists will edit, replace words, correct grammar, and leave out seemingly redundant comments. As well-meaning as these efforts may be, they can be detrimental to the analysis. Verification can be done quickly. Spot-check your transcripts at several random locations. Start at the beginning of the tape recording and match the words to the transcript. Then skip ahead to several places in the tape and again match the transcript to the actual words. If a discrepancy occurs, you may need to prepare another transcript.

If you analyze a focus group that you didn't attend, it is valuable to listen to the tape while reading the transcript. Some factors important to analysis won't appear on the transcript, but you may be able to detect them on the tape recordings. These include expressions of intensity, humor, or excitement.

Flip Charts and Response Forms

Flip charts and all response forms completed by participants can be useful in analysis. Flip charts, which are prepared by the moderator during the group discussion, can be helpful in capturing the range of participant responses, in tabulating results of response forms, or in summarizing differing points of view. The flip chart allows participants to observe what is being recorded and, if necessary, to modify, revise, or verify those comments. Following the focus group, these flip charts are helpful in retrieving the key points.

There can be quite a variety of response forms used in a focus group: rating sheets, sentence completions, listings of characteristics, semantic differential rating sheets, sketches, and so on. All of these are important to collect for later analysis. These forms are used primarily as stimuli to promote later discussion, but often they are tabulated and analyzed as well.

Another type of data is the registration forms completed by participants at the beginning of the focus group. It is from these forms that we are able to obtain background information, such as occupation, educational level, income, past experience with a program or product, and so forth. These demographic and usage characteristics can be helpful in understanding comments and opinions shared within the focus group.

Computer

Computers can be used in a number of ways to assist with focus group analysis. Perhaps the most obvious is the preparation of transcripts. The researcher can sort, categorize, and rearrange statements with ease. In addition, the computer provides the opportunity to add participant names or create wide margins for notes or coding. In some situations, it may be possible to transcribe during the focus group interview using a laptop computer. Recently, several computer programs have been created to help with the analysis process. These programs don't actually perform the analysis but rather retrieve sections that have been previously coded by the analyst.

More Discussion of Computer Analysis Appears in Chapter 3 and in Chapter 8

Long Table, Scissors, and Colored Marking Pens

Finally, we would be remiss if we did not talk about the classic tools for analysis—long tables (or the living room floor), scissors, and marking pens. This low-technology option has been used in countless analysis projects, and it allows the analyst to identify themes and categorize results. It does not look elegant, it eats up table (or floor) space for the duration of the analysis, and it looks chaotic—but it works. The equipment needs are simple: a long table (lots of floor space will substitute nicely, if you don't mind bending down), scissors, and colored marking pens (or colored stick-on notes), colored paper for printing the reports, and flip charts or large sheets of paper.

This strategy can operate in a variety of ways and is limited only by your creativity. When I've used the "long table" approach, here is how I operate.

I begin by gathering transcripts or abridged transcripts. I make two copies of each document, one to cut up and one that stays intact. I then arrange these transcripts in a reasonable order. It could be in the sequence in which the groups were conducted, but more likely it will be by categories of participants or by some demographic screening characteristics (users, nonusers, and employees; teens, young adults, and older adults; etc.). This arrangement helps me be alert to changes that may be occurring from one group to another.

I've found that colored paper and colored markers are helpful for keeping track of different categories. After cutting up sections and taping quotes together, it is easy to forget the source of the quotes. At times, this source information is vital to analysis. As a solution, I print transcripts on different colors of paper, thereby color-coding the transcripts by audience type, category, and so on (e.g., teenagers on blue paper and parents on green paper). At other times, I use colored marking pens, highlight pens, or stick-on notes to identify quotes that are cut out.

Before I begin cutting, I do a quick reading of all transcripts. Typically, I've already read these, and this quick reading is just to remind myself of the whole scope and to refresh my memory of where information is located, what information is missing, and what information occurs in abundance. If I haven't read them all, I set aside some time and read everything, taking notes about ideas, themes, word choices, and other items.

I place flip charts or large sheets of paper on long tables or the floor. At the top of the newsprint pages, I identify a question or theme. Now it's time to begin the cutting and taping. I've learned the importance of documenting the source of every quote; later, I may want to go back and examine the context of a particular discussion, and this source information is vital. Sometimes, I divide the newsprint page into categories to represent different types of focus group participants. For example, on one part of the page, I place comments from teen focus groups, on another, comments from parent focus groups, and on a third, comments from teacher focus groups.

Soon my paper is filling up with participant quotes. After I've placed everything into categories, I'm ready to begin analysis of specific themes or questions. Not everything necessarily fits neatly into categories. I've found that, in focus groups, people get off topic or expand in detail on an aspect of minimal importance to the study. I don't toss this material. Instead, I save it in the event that it is needed later. Sometimes, I rearrange the categories, create new categories, or just recheck the storage areas for unused quotes.

Now I look over each category and write descriptive summaries of each section. What is similar and what is different about the comments? I think about whether I want simply to describe or to go further and offer an interpretation, or even a recommendation, for each theme or question.

When I am finished placing items in categories and developing descriptions, I take a break and refocus on the big picture.

What prompted the study? It's easy to get sidetracked into areas of minor importance. Then, after a while, I conclude the analysis by arranging the report based on the purpose of the study and the areas of greatest importance.

The long table approach is still quite effective. Quite a number of variations are possible, but the core elements are basically cutting, sorting, and arranging.

7

Questions Focus Group Analysts Must Face

Overview

Questions Asked of Focus Group Researchers

Questions Asked by Focus Group Researchers

Y ou are going to get questions. Some questions will be about the topic under investigation, and others will be about focus groups as a research method. Questions come from colleagues, sponsors, interested individuals, focus group participants, and sometimes skeptics. A few questions will be vexing because they come at the time of reporting instead of at the time of planning, when they should have been addressed. During the oral report, you are intent on sharing your findings, but instead, questions emerge about the methodology. The vexing questions aren't about results but about the research procedures and the philosophical underpinnings of the study. Here is what you might do when you encounter these questions.

First, anticipate questions. By anticipating questions, you can think through your answers to maximize clarity and conciseness.

Anticipating questions begins with being thoughtful about your audience. What experience have they had with this study and similar studies? Are they familiar with focus group studies in general? What is their degree of engagement or commitment to the study? What are their expectations of the report?

Think about the traditions of the organization and the environment of the report. In some situations, you as a reporter take on a role of presenting and responding to challenges, which is associated with academic meetings and professional associations. Another tradition is the hierarchical model in which the study has been "blessed and approved" by top management, tough questions have already been asked in the planning stage, and the audience is now expected to applaud and cheer the results. Still another is an environment in which the audience is expected to take action based on the findings, and the questions asked are intended to help managers convey findings and action steps to subordinates. In this case, the questions asked of the reporter are the questions that middle managers anticipate being asked themselves. In effect, this is a train-the-trainer model on answering questions. These are some differences we've seen, but more undoubtedly exist. The way you answer will depend on these circumstances. The degree of detail and the manner of response will differ slightly in each environment.

Second, consider the reason for the question. Don't assume that the question necessarily reflects a desire for information. Ask yourself, why is this question being asked? You probably won't be certain of the reasons, but you will have a hunch that is based on past questions, the context of the report, or the person asking the question. We've seen several types of questioners.

- Some who ask questions truly want answers. They are curious and interested in what you are doing. They may have struggled themselves and are eager to learn new strategies and skills. These individuals may want more information about particular findings or the future uses of the study. *Response strategy*: Give the answer as best you can, invite someone else to answer, or postpone the answer until later.

- Some will ask questions, but they are really making statements. It may be a statement for or against your study or a statement on an entirely different topic. Don't assume that you need to have an answer. *Response strategy*: Thank the person for the comment and continue with other questions.

- Some ask questions to fill time, to appear polite, to seem interested in the study, or even to help you. *Response strategy:* Answer the question, invite someone else to answer, or postpone the answer until later.

- For some, the questions are the beginning of a trap. They are seeking to find fault or to expose a perceived inadequacy of the study. Be cautious of the two-part question. The first part may seem innocent, but the second part can be deadly. *Response strategy:* State or repeat the rationale for the study and why the methodology was deemed appropriate. Describe the systematic procedures. Clarify the limitations.

NOTE: A strategy that we discourage is to answer a different question. The researcher might change the question to one he or she can answer and then answer that revised question. Sometimes, this is done inadvertently, as when the question isn't understood and an attempt is made to provide an answer. Other times, the strategy is an overt attempt to switch the question to one that the respondent is able to answer. This strategy is not advised.

Sometimes, questions reflect beliefs that someone holds about the nature of research and the scientific method. These beliefs are developed by reading and study, by the influence of others such as teachers and professors who tell us what is the proper and acceptable way of knowing, and by experience.

For some, research approaches are like religious beliefs. Religious groups hold a variety of views. Some contend that they alone have the correct answers and approaches to life's problems. Another view is that, while other beliefs exist and these other beliefs may be worthy, the approach of their own community of faith is the most correct way. Still others hold multiple views, not seeing any belief system as exclusive and even holding to the view that one can hold different beliefs simultaneously.

In your travels as a researcher, you'll likely encounter people who hold each of these views. Occasionally, some will have a conversion experience, an epiphany, or a slow changing of beliefs, but it is unlikely that this will occur during your research presentation. Therefore, be respectful of alternative views, and don't attempt to persuade people to abandon their past beliefs. This is not the moment for conversion.

Let's begin by examining questions that are about qualitative or focus group research methodology. At some point, you will be asked questions such as these. Note that your answers will need to be tailored to the specific situation. Here are some questions that we've heard and our answers. First, we discuss questions that are asked of focus group researchers by others. We suggest answers that we've used and also some additional background and thoughts about the answers that you may wish to consider. Second, we present questions asked by focus group researchers.

Questions Asked of Focus Group Researchers

Here are questions that are regularly asked of focus group researchers.

Q. Is This Scientific Research?

A. The goal of qualitative research is to understand and communicate, not to control or replicate a study. These qualitative research methods are accepted by researchers, and researchers in all fields are increasingly discovering the benefit of multiple methods of research. The issue is not if these methods represent scientific research, but, rather, whether this mix of research methods is appropriate for the situation at hand.

Background

For decades, social scientists have sought to improve the quality of their research by perfecting scientific procedures. They found the experimental design strategies used in physical and biological sciences to be instructive and helpful. During this time, the strategies of randomization, control groups, and experimental designs became popular and accepted. However, scientists were soon disappointed, for although they learned a great deal, they found that this positivistic approach to scientific research actually limited their thinking and overlooked valuable data. Consequently, other scientific procedures emerged that also proved to be applicable to social science inquiry. Various names were given to these scientific procedures, but in general, they belong to a category called qualitative research.

Thoughts

This question regularly comes from someone who has been told that there is only one right way to conduct scientific research, and that way is a positivistic method. Too often, when we think of scientific research, we limit ourselves to thinking about control groups, randomization, and experimental design. The approach that has been well established is that of positivism, whereby we set hypotheses, control the experiment, and then project to a population. We owe a great deal to the traditions of logical-positivistic scientific methods. Many major discoveries and beneficial changes can be attributed to this style of research and way of knowing. In fact, this way of thinking is so traditional and predominant within the United States that we often overlook other ways of knowing and conducting research.

Q. Isn't Focus Group Research Just Subjective Opinions?

A. We've approached this study recognizing the importance of two guiding principles: researcher neutrality and systematic procedures. We've addressed researcher neutrality in several ways. The research was conducted by a team of people with differing backgrounds to ensure that the results presented reflect multiple perspectives. Our research team was aware of the need for neutrality and the importance of capturing all participant views. For each point identified in our results, we have established a trail of evidence that can be verified.

Throughout the study, we've used accepted systematic procedures for data collection, data handling, and data analysis. We've used field notes and electronic recordings to capture the comments, which were then reviewed and used in the analysis process. During the focus group, we would ask participants to explain their views if we did not clearly understand what was said. Then, following the discussion, we offered a summary of key findings that participants verified. Our later debriefing and reports involved a team approach. Our analysis used accepted systematic steps of identifying key points, followed by comparing results with those of other groups in order to identify patterns. Because we've used these procedures, we have confidence that what is presented is an accurate reflection of the focus group participants' views.

Background

A study that is subjective is one in which researchers are so close and familiar with the study that their judgment is affected. Such results cannot be trusted because they are influenced by personal judgment and opinion, which are subject to error.

Objectivity, on the other hand, makes use of instruments or standardized procedures that measure precisely something without human influence. These instruments have been used in past studies and seek to precisely measure the phenomenon under investigation.

Some may feel that objective measures are superior because objective measures are better indicators. In fact, what is seen as an objective (or hard) indicator can be wrong. If these measures are wrong, then the results and analysis that follow will also be wrong. For example, if you limit the response categories or crudely force complex concepts into simplistic statements, the results are clearly subject to error.

Thoughts

It is hard to judge the intent of this question. Sometimes, this is a friendly question where the questioner wishes to help the researcher. Other times, this is a cynical question implying disrespect for certain types of research. Therefore, give thought as to how you answer. Be respectful and honoring of other points of view or other research philosophies, even if others do not show respect for your views. Avoid becoming defensive as you give your answer.

Avoid words such as *subjective* versus *objective,* or *soft* versus *hard.* These questions are often a reflection of someone's belief in research. Quite often, these questions assume that certain types of research are superior to others. Some types of research are called "objective" or "hard," and these types are deemed to be more scientific and, hence, more accurate and better.

CHECKLIST

**Tips for
Answering
Questions on
Subjectivity**

☐ *Don't be surprised.*
☐ *Be respectful.*
☐ *Don't get defensive.*
☐ *Assume the questioner really wants an answer.*
☐ *Tell how people worked together to ensure neutrality.*
☐ *Describe how data were captured.*
☐ *Describe how data were verified.*
☐ *Describe how data were analyzed.*

Now, do all of the above in less than 2 minutes!

Q. Isn't This Soft Research?

A. When referring to research, the words "soft" and "hard" lack the clarity that scientists need to describe their research inquiry. These terms tend to foster confusion and inaccuracy, and therefore they are typically not used. Focus group interviews are a respected form of scientific research when the procedures are systematic and the results are verifiable. Focus group research is not "anything you want it to be."

Background

The words *soft* or *hard* referring to research are imprecise and misleading. It is unclear what makes one type of data hard and another soft, for indeed, people have approached this question differently. *Hard* tends to refer to numbers, especially those coming from standardized sources of testing, measurement, surveys, or experimental design. On the other hand, *soft* refers to data that come from people in conditions that are variable and changeable, such as descriptive, observational, or interview situations. Increasingly, scientists are avoiding these terms. The colloquial language of *hard research* and *soft research* is pejorative, simplistic, and sometimes inflammatory for these words imply a superior-subordinate relationship.

Thoughts

It's easy to get defensive on this question. It is also difficult to determine just why this question is asked. Sometimes, questioners are just curious about how you might answer, for perhaps they've been asked the question and want to know how to respond. Other times, they really want to make a point about what is "good" or "acceptable" research. The context is important in helping you decide how to answer.

An alternative answer might be to describe the systematic nature of focus group research along with the ability to verify results. Review the description in Chapter 2 of systematic and verifiable analysis.

Yet another way to answer is to discuss the value of observing but not interfering with the population. This means a lack of control. In positivistic research, the emphasis is placed on achieving control. Research is "hard" if it uses sufficient controls that document what has happened. The environment is controlled, people are controlled in terms of what treatment they receive, and the variables that affect the study are also controlled. Many human environments, outside of the laboratory, cannot and should not be controlled.

Q. How Do You Determine Validity?

A. Our research team was concerned about the quality of the information and that the results be a valid reflection of how the participants felt and thought about the topic. We've taken several steps to ensure the validity of the results.

We've pilot tested the questions to ensure that they were understood. We've listened to participants in advance of the study to provide the conditions needed for free and open sharing. We've used a team of moderators who were appropriate for the situation. We've listened carefully to participants, observed how they answered, and sought clarification on areas of ambiguity. Then, at the conclusion of the focus group, we asked participants to verify our summary comments. In summary, we've followed the accepted protocol to ensure that our results are trustworthy and valid.

Background

Essentially, this is a question about trusting your results. In the positivistic or quantitative tradition, it has been important to determine validity, because a test or instrument was created to measure something, and it would occasionally measure the wrong thing. Furthermore, sometimes that instrument would accurately measure a phenomenon for which the test would be valid, but the test would be invalid for another situation. For example, an instrument might be a valid measure of student teacher knowledge and skills but be an invalid measure of future teacher success.

In these quantitative studies, the instrument was a proxy for what was really measured. By contrast, in focus group research, there are no proxies. The actual words of participants, not instruments, are used to find out their feelings, thoughts, or observations about the topic of discussion. Moreover, the researcher is able to draw on multiple sources of information that are not normally available to the quantitative researcher. The focus group researcher observes the answers and has the opportunity to follow up and probe to amplify or clarify the response. In addition, the focus group researcher can report the key points and seek verification from participants.

Thoughts

The challenge to focus group validity is real but lies in another place. The threat is the potential for false findings, deceptiveness, or dissembling for whatever reason. For example, participants will sometimes hold back because of perceived threats or group pressure; other times, they will exaggerate in order to impress or convince. The challenge to the researcher is whether to trust what was said, and then for the user to trust the findings of the researcher.

Focus groups are unique in qualitative research because of their group nature. Groups offer advantages and disadvantages. There can be subtle pressure to conform and to agree with others. In other situations, the individual may feel that it is not proper to discuss a topic in front of a group or may have fears about who is listening and how the information might be used.

To determine validity, the researcher must look at the larger context of the study and see the study from the perspective of the participants. In some sensitive situations, many factors can influence the validity of what is said: something about the moderator (race, age, gender, knowledge, etc.), the presence of a one-way mirror, a perception that the topic is private versus public, a past history of consequences to people who've shared concerns, the trust that the results are confidential, or a host of other concerns.

These concerns ought to be considered in the planning stages. When in doubt, ask a number of potential participants for their advice on how best to create an open environment for discussion. Were the focus groups truly permissive and non-threatening? Did the moderator use caution in guiding the group to avoid group pressure and offer each individual adequate opportunity to share his or her views?

Q. Can You Generalize?

A. This study is not intended to generalize. Focus group research is conducted to gain a more complete understanding of a particular topic, such as motivation, behavior, feelings, decision-making strategies, or just how certain people think about an issue or topic. Our goal is to go "in-depth" into a topic, and therefore, we spend a considerable amount of time conducting research with a small number of people. Other research methods, by contrast, do not go "in-depth" but use close-ended questions with limited response choices that offer breadth instead of depth. These studies that offer breadth are the ones used to make generalizations.

So, in a strict sense, one cannot generalize, but what we suggest is the concept of transferability. That is, a person who wants to use the results should give thought about whether or not the findings can transfer into another environment. This decision is made by examining the research methods, the audience, and the context and by considering if these situations and conditions are sufficiently similar to the new environment. What we suggest is that you consider our methods, procedures, and audience and decide the degree to which these results fit the situation you face.

Background

Transferability, according to Guba and Lincoln (1989), is parallel to the positivistic concept of generalizability, except that it is the receiver (not the sender or researcher) who decides if the results can be applied to the next situation. The person reviewing the research looks over the conditions, the environment, and procedures and then decides the degree of fit for the second situation.

Thoughts

For More Information, See *Fourth Generation Evaluation* **by Egon Guba and Yvonna Lincoln**

When you present focus group results, questions will regularly occur about the ability to generalize. To some, the greatest goal of research is to have control and to be able to predict what might happen next. You can see that this approach would have considerable popularity in the biological and physical sciences.

Generalizability is a nifty concept, but if you are really intending to understand, describe, or interpret, then the quest for generalizability might lead you astray.

Through randomization and adequate sampling, the positivistic researcher is able to promise generalizability. With generalizability, the researcher describes the degree to which these results are expected to occur in other places. By contrast, focus group research involves only a limited number of people who may not be selected in a random manner. As a result, this promise of generalizability is untenable.

Therefore, don't promise generalizability. Suggest instead that those who seek to use the results look over the study; examine the procedures, methods, and analysis strategies; and then decide the degree to which the study might be applied to their situation. What may be transferred are the larger theoretical concepts, as opposed to the specific behaviors.

Q. Why Don't You Use Random Sampling?

A. Because random sampling is not always appropriate. Instead, in focus group research, the strategy is to use "purposeful" sampling, whereby the researcher selects participants based on the purpose of the study. For example, the research might be to study users of a program, teenagers in the community who have experienced violence, or diabetic men over the age of 50. In each situation, we are seeking out these kinds of people because they have special knowledge or experiences that are helpful in the study. They are what Patton (1990) calls "information-rich" cases. Focus groups are composed of homogeneous groups of people with something in common that is relevant to the topic of study. In these cases, random sampling of the population would be a waste of time and resources. However, the researcher often assembles a pool of potential participants and then selects randomly from within this pool of qualified individuals. This level of randomization is regularly done, and it helps minimize selection bias.

Background

Be able to give the logic as cited by experts. Consider looking over the following:

Basics of qualitative research (1990) by Anselm Strauss and Juliet Corbin. Review Chapter 11 on theoretical sampling.

The discovery of grounded theory (1967) by Barney Glaser and Anselm Strauss. Note discussions of theoretical sampling.

Qualitative evaluation and research methods (1990) by Michael Quinn Patton. Sage. Read Chapter 5 on designing qualitative studies.

Thoughts

In quantitative research considerable attention is paid to random sampling. The reason is that randomization helps ensure that a sample is a snapshot of the larger population. The quality of the sample is determined by size and randomness. If the size is too small and the sample not random, the quality will be suspect. Therefore, it is no surprise that quantitative researchers are concerned about the size and randomness of focus group studies.

Q. How Big Is the Sample? or How Can You Make Those Statements With Such a Small Sample?

A. In this form of research, the quality of the study is not dependent on the size of the sample. The intent is to achieve "theoretical saturation," which is akin to redundancy. We are watching for patterns in our interview results, and we will sample until we discover that we have "saturated" the theory or found redundant information. In focus group research, the rule of thumb has been to conduct three or four focus groups for a particular audience and then decide if additional groups (or cases) should be added to the study. Large-scale studies with the divergent populations often require more groups, but our goal is to determine the variability of a concept or idea.

Background

Michael Patton offers an example that might be helpful in your answer.

> Piaget contributed a major breakthrough to our understanding of how children think by observing his own two children at length and in great depth. Freud established the field of psychoanalysis based on fewer than ten client cases. Bandler and Grinder founded neurolinguistic programming by studying three re-nowned and highly effective therapists. . . . Peters and Waterman formulated their widely followed eight principles for organizational excellence by studying 62 companies, a very small sample of the thousands of companies one might study.
> The validity, meaningfulness, and insights generated from qualitative inquiry have more to do with the information-richness of the cases selected and the observational/analytical capabilities of the researcher than with sample size. (Patton, 1990, p. 185)

Thoughts

Small sample size will be hard for some researchers to swallow. Quantitative research procedures have repeatedly called for randomization and adequate sample size. Indeed, sample size is a criterion of quality in quantitative research. The logic of sampling in qualitative research is different. The sample type and size are determined by the purpose of the study and the nature of what is discovered.

Questions Asked by Focus Group Researchers

Here are questions asked by beginning researchers themselves.

Q. How Do I Capture Information?

A. The choices are memory, field notes, audiotape, videotape, and real-time transcription. Use as many methods as you can afford. Multiple methods are preferred.

Q. Should I Analyze by Questions or Themes?

A. In focus group analysis, you can proceed in two general ways. The easiest for beginning moderators is to analyze question by question, looking for themes within questions and then across questions (e.g., What themes emerge from the responses to question 3? Are there themes that cut across questions?). The second way is to organize the results around themes—themes that are developed either before, during, or after the focus groups. This approach will be discussed a bit more in Chapter 11. Reflect on which strategy best accomplishes the purpose of the study.

Q. Should I Edit Messy Quotations?

A. People very rarely talk in crisp statements that result in insightful quotations. In real life, people use incomplete sentences or ramble along with disconnected thoughts strung together with verbal pauses. Thus, transcripts of focus group interviews inevitably contain messy quotations. The researcher must determine the extent to which statements should be abridged or modified. Often, only a portion of the statement is critical to capture the intent of the speaker. An area where editing is often needed is in the placement of periods. Run-on sentences that are understood when spoken may get confusing when read. A period often improves readability.

It is essential in editing quotations that the researcher captures the intended meaning of the speaker. Sometimes, the actual words do not convey the meaning—as in situations where the speaker is trying to use humor or irony and will say the opposite of what is intended. The researcher has an obligation to present the views of the participants fairly and accurately. To fulfill this obligation, some minor editing to correct grammar is appropriate as long as the meaning is not changed.

Generally, we correct grammar but do not change the words. We may add a word or phrase and place it within a parenthesis. This occurs when all participants in the focus group knew what the topic was. To the reader of the statement, however, it may not be obvious.

Q. How Should I Interpret Nonverbal Communication?

A. Nonverbal communication can easily be overlooked in the analysis, especially when the researcher relies only on transcripts. The researcher should consider the energy level or enthusiasm within the group. Enthusiastic comments and excitement for the topic should be factored into statements of the findings. Also note the degree of spontaneity and the extent of participant involvement. Spontaneous comments, where probing is unneeded, may signal that people are interested in the idea. In addition, the researcher should be attentive to body language expressed during the group session. The moderator and assistant moderator should make notes of the nonverbal responses during the actual interview session; these are then considered when analyzing the results. We favor a conservative approach in interpreting body language because it can mean different things. Body language provides merely a first clue, and verbal confirmation is needed before incorporating the concept into the analysis.

Q. How Should I Report Numbers in Focus Group Results?

A. Numbers and percentages ought to be used with caution in the focus group report. Numbers sometimes convey the impression that results can be projected to a population, and this is not within the capabilities of qualitative research procedures. Instead, the researcher might consider the use of more descriptive phrases, such as "the prevalent feeling was . . . ," "several participants strongly felt that . . . ," or even "most participants agreed that . . . ."

Q. What's Done With Information That Comes After the Focus Group?

A. Sometimes, the researcher receives information that is relevant to the topic, but it is obtained after the focus group interview has concluded. In one-to-one interviewing, this is often a nonissue because the interview may not have a defined moment of closure. The focus group is different because in focus groups, the individuals have the opportunity to hear other views and to respond. As a result, comments made after the group has adjourned cannot be countered or amplified by other individuals. When deciding what to do with this information, the researcher might consider one of the primary rules of social science research: Don't disregard any information. Make note of the comment, but also describe the circumstances under which it was received. The decision to use the information in analysis and reporting is another matter. The prudent researcher will use care in handling this late-arriving information. In making the decision to use it, the researcher might consider the reason for the delay. In some cases, it might simply be an afterthought of a participant on the way out of the focus group. In other situations, a participant might be inhibited or anxious about sharing a controversial view and choose to communicate to the researcher in private. This late-arriving information may have special meaning, and the researcher could well inquire about the reason for the delay.

Essentially, there are three choices for what to do with this information. First, use it like any other information from the focus group, treating it in the same manner as the focus group data. The second strategy is to use the information in the analysis but to note that it was said after the group. The third choice is to collect the information and treat it as background information not to be included or mentioned in the report. We've favored the second approach, but on occasion, we have opted for the third choice.

Q. Should I Ever Exclude or Ignore Information?

A. Yes, but this occurs in the analysis stage, not in the data collection stage. Occasionally, the analyst will choose purposely to set aside information or comments in the focus group. In analysis, this occurs because the analyst seeks to discover and bring to the surface those concepts that are most relevant to the purpose of the study. The process of analysis requires data reduction and selective attention to certain topics. Not every story or experience told is relevant. Even if they are relevant, not all stories need to be shared to give the reader an understanding of the point. The purpose of the study drives what is included.

Occasionally, the analyst gets more information than intended. Sometimes, people tell experiences in greater detail than is expected or needed. Participants may talk about other people, employers, customers, or others, in negative and demeaning terms. Other times, the participants tell about their behaviors or experiences, and if shared publicly, these could prove to be harmful or detrimental to the participants. Confidentiality was promised. This means that no names are attached to reports and that the speaker cannot be identified by other situational or contextual factors.

Q. Who Should Analyze Focus Group Data?

A. Often, the best choice is the moderator or assistant moderator, if these individuals have skills in analysis. The moderator or assistant has the advantage of actually having been present in the focus group. This makes the analysis easier and less time-consuming. Traditionally, in focus group research, the moderator is also the analyst. However, when working with nonprofit and public organizations, sometimes the moderator is a volunteer or a staff person, and the analysis is conducted by a focus group professional.

Sometimes, the analysis task is shared by the moderator, the assistant moderator, and an experienced researcher-analyst. In these cases, the moderator and the assistant are often asked to use their field notes, listen to the audiotape, and prepare a brief analysis of each focus group. This task often consists of preparing a summary for each question, along with selected notable quotes. The analyst will usually work closely with the moderator(s) and assistant(s) and involve them in the discovery of themes across the series of focus groups.

Another choice is for all analysis to be completed by an experienced researcher, even if the researcher was not present in the groups. This is clearly a difficult task for the researcher. In order to take on this task, the researcher should obtain as much of the data stream as possible, including transcripts, audiotapes, and field notes. To make this task more manageable, it is often helpful for the analyst to interview the moderators and assistants who were present in the groups. Even with all this information, the farther the analyst is from the actual experience of the groups, the harder it is to do a high-quality analysis.

8

Strategies Used by Experts

Overview

I've invited several experts to share their strategies for focus group analysis. Note that they use different strategies and procedures. Some strategies are regularly used, but others are not. All of these individuals are masters at analysis. They consistently produce top-quality results. Give thought to their suggestions.

The experts are the following:

Mary Anne Casey, a focus group moderator and evaluation consultant in Minneapolis-St. Paul, Minnesota. She works primarily with not-for-profit organizations. I've watched her analyze focus groups and found that she has a special gift in listening, analyzing, and reporting.

Reyn Kinzey, Vice President, Kinzey & Day Qualitative Market Research, in Richmond, Virginia. He is also a member of the adjunct faculty for the English Department at Virginia Commonwealth University. Through workshops, presentations, and articles, he has helped focus group moderators across the country on practical strategies for analysis and reporting.

David L. Morgan, a professor at Portland State University, Portland, Oregon. A sociologist by training, he has keen insight into the human condition, a scholar's eye for detail, and the wisdom that comes from academic research. He offers two strategies for consideration.

Marilyn J. Rausch, a focus group moderator in Minneapolis-St. Paul, Minnesota. She has traveled throughout the country conducting hundreds of focus groups on a wide variety of topics. She has taught focus group moderating, coached beginning moderators, and is regularly sought out by other moderators for advice and counsel.

Analysis—Honoring the Stories
by Mary Anne Casey

I work with not-for-profit agencies, which usually means no money for rooms with one-way mirrors. This, in turn, means the people interested in the results often don't get a chance to experience the groups firsthand. They don't get a chance to feel the delight, concern, pain, or indifference. They don't get to hear people describe what they like or don't like. They don't see what makes people angry or what gives them hope. They don't hear the stories. So I become their storyteller. My role is to honor what people have shared and present it to the sponsor of the study in a way that is useful.

When I first started analyzing focus groups, I used the same process over and over. It didn't matter what the study was about, how complex the topic was, how much money was in the budget, or how many groups were being done. I didn't stray from this process. It gave me structure, which gave me courage to wade into the messiness of analysis. I always knew how to start, and I always started as soon as the first group ended so I never had to face a pile of unanalyzed tapes. And I only dealt with manageable chunks of data. It made the thought of doing analysis less overwhelming.

Here is the process I have often used:

- I participate in the groups as the moderator or assistant moderator. For me, being present in the group makes analysis much easier. I have a feel for the gist of the group, which is lost if I only listen to the tapes.
- I type an abbreviated transcript as soon as possible after each group. I listen to the tape, and for each question, I transcribe only the comments that might be useful in analysis. I don't type the introduction. I don't type anything that is off track. I don't type the "uh-huhs," "yeah," or "you knows." I boldface all of the questions so they are easy to find. I use the cut-and-paste function on the word processor to move text to the appropriate question. (For example, if responses to question five are really answers to question seven, I move that text under question seven.)

    As I listen to tapes, I ask myself:
    Does the information answer the question?
    What can I say about the responses to this question
    in a report?
    How useful is the information?
    Based on the purpose of the study, what else would I
    want to know if I were the sponsor?
- I try to finish each transcript before conducting the next group. It is amazing how this can improve moderating. While transcribing, I often catch things I didn't catch while I was moderating.

    I may realize the participants never really answered the question, so I know I need to make sure they answer the question in following groups. Example: In recent groups with university faculty members, I asked them what their college should focus on in the next 5 years. They had a rousing conversation. It wasn't until I listened to the tape that I noticed the conversation was about the lack of direction of the college leadership, rather than which direction the participants thought the college should go.

    Or I may realize that the group is interpreting a question in an unintended way, so we need to re-phrase the question. Example: A health-care system was trying to improve care of patients with chronic depression. The sponsor wanted to find out family members' perceptions of how family members were involved in the patients' care. We asked family members, "How involved do you feel you've been in your family member's care?" When listening to the tapes, I realized that family members thought the question was about how involved they were in caring for the patient on a day-to-day basis while at home, rather than about how health-care professionals had involved family members in the treatment process.

Or I may discover that a theme is developing and that I need to explore this theme more deeply with the next groups. Example: In the same study of how to improve the care of people with major depression, we asked patients what they looked for in a caregiver. Over and over, people said, "someone who listens" and "someone who cares." In later groups, I pressed participants to give examples of what caregivers did that showed they cared or that they were listening and, in reverse, what caregivers did that showed they weren't listening or didn't care.

- If the sponsor wants a written summary of each group, I will write a short (one- to two-page) bulleted summary after I have completed the abbreviated transcript. The summary may list key points or may contain a two- to three-sentence summary of responses to each question. I also include recommendations for changes to the following focus groups based on what we learned in this group.

- After I have completed a series of transcripts, I start to analyze systematically across groups. Sometimes, I just get all the transcripts around me, read them looking for patterns and trends, and highlight quotes I want to use. Other times, I merge the computer files of the transcripts and then move all the answers to question one from all the groups to the same spot. I continue for each question. I end up with a master transcript—one document containing all the relevant responses. This way, I can look at one text rather than flipping through three or four transcripts. I examine all the responses to a particular question looking for patterns, trends, or themes across responses. I move quotes that illustrate a particular theme together. Then I write a paragraph summarizing that theme. Then I move down the list of questions. When using a master transcript, I delete quotes I don't want to use, rather than highlighting quotes I want.

- During this process, these kinds of questions run through my head:

    > What are people saying?
    >
    > What are people feeling?
    >
    > What is really important?
    >
    > What are the themes?
    >
    > How do the groups compare?
    >
    > Are there any gems or bits of wisdom that were said only once but deserve to be noted?
    >
    > Which quotes really give the essence of the conversation?
    >
    > What will be useful to the sponsor?

- Before I am done analyzing across groups in this question-by-question process, I begin to struggle with how to present what was heard in a meaningful way. What are the over-arching themes or messages? What does all this mean? How should it be presented? I don't really know how to describe how I do this. It is the art of analysis. Sometimes, I know immediately what and how to share what was learned. Other times, I walk around for days, even weeks, moving data through my head, mulling over what was said, waiting for inspiration to strike—to discover a categorization scheme, story line, or format that really describes what we learned from the groups. When it happens, I know.

- When I have prepared a written or oral report, I ask myself if it really reflects what participants said. I want to honor what they shared and be true to them.

- It may sound like I'm the Lone Ranger when it comes to analysis. I'm not. Throughout the process, I have sounding boards nearby—perhaps colleagues or assistant moderators who know the study. I can describe a finding, share my perspective on it, and ask for theirs. Additional filters or perspectives can be immensely helpful. In addition, I share what I have heard and my perceptions with the sponsor along the way. That way, I can make sure I am gathering information that is helpful to them.

Although this is the process that I often use, I do modify it.

- I don't always use transcripts. Although a part of me still wonders if I have given a study adequate attention if I don't use transcripts, another part is secure in knowing that most sponsors want and expect a small number of key points, and these points can be found without sifting through hundreds of pages of quotes. I've found that key points usually resurface and repeat in various parts of the focus group.

- Sometimes, I use flip chart notes and field notes as a basis for a group summary. If I know a sponsor wants a summary of each group very quickly (like the day after each group), I take more notes on the flip chart during the group. There just isn't time to wait for a transcription as a basis for a summary.

- Sometimes, I use transcripts others have typed. Although I believe typing my own transcripts has made me a better moderator, I hate transcribing. Also, it isn't cost-effective for me to do it. So, these days, I often have someone else transcribe if transcripts are needed.

- Sometimes, I use only the assistant moderator's notes as a basis for analysis. I now know that different studies call for different degrees of analysis. Not every focus group study needs transcripts.

- Sometimes, I use transcripts for some groups and field notes for other groups in the same study. Recently, we conducted 16 groups for a study: four groups in each of four cities. The budget didn't allow for transcripts of all groups, but we felt some transcription would improve analysis. After completing a set of groups in a city, we would decide which two of the four groups would be transcribed. We then used a combination of transcripts and field notes for analysis.

- Sometimes, I use a moderator debriefing session and field notes as the basis for analysis. Sometimes, we have multiple moderators involved in the same study. As part of the analysis process, we convene the moderators at the completion of the groups and ask them to share what they heard in response to each of the questions. We ask them to compare and contrast groups. We ask them to provide verbatim quotes from their notes that illustrate the points. We ask them for their interpretations and what they see are the key points of the study. Then we use this as the basis for analysis.

The key to analysis is to know what will be useful to the sponsor. Once I understand the quest from the sponsors' perspective, then my job is to sort through the data to unearth or highlight the information that will be most helpful to them. So I always begin analysis with a clear understanding of the problem. Then I pass all information through a mental screen of "does this help solve the problem?"

For quite a while, my analysis consisted of describing what was said. I thought it was enough. It usually seemed so self-explanatory. Now I push myself to give my interpretation of what it means and to share what I think might be done based on what I heard.

Report Writing Without Guilt
by Reyn Kinzey

Many moderators, including some of the best and most experienced in the business, tell me they hate writing reports. They never question the importance of the reports—to provide a historical record of the findings, state recommendations, and provide a sense of closure to the project. They just hate writing them.

Some of that dread is understandable. The skills of a good moderator are not necessarily the same as those of a good report writer—moderators are extroverted, verbal people, while writers are often introverted, literary (visual) people. Nevertheless, I would argue that moderators already have the essential skills to be good, competent report writers: They are trained to be good listeners who hear people on their own terms; they can summarize what they hear; and they have the intuitive sense of where to go next in a conversation, and, by extension, in a research project. If moderators would allow themselves to think more clearly about the process of report writing, including an honest appreciation of the strengths and limitations of qualitative market research, I think most of them could write reports without so much anxiety and, perhaps just as importantly in today's competitive environment, more quickly.

First, we need to remember that the kind of qualitative research I am discussing here—focus groups and one-on-ones—is first and foremost based on people's self-reports of their own behavior and attitudes. We are not psychoanalysts. Our first duty is to report what people have said about their own behavior and attitudes. As a moderator, I believe as much as the next person in reading body language and paying attention to what is not said as well as to what is said. However, as a report writer, I finally have to report what was said. If I was able, as a moderator, to use "negative body language" to probe more deeply into what participants "were really thinking," then, good for me; I can use what I got from those probes in the report. If I didn't manage such effective probing, any speculation I might offer on "what they were really thinking" is just that: speculation. It doesn't have any place in the report.

This reliance on participants' self-reports of their behavior and attitudes is a great strength of qualitative research. It is a correcting influence on advertisers, product designers, service providers, and even politicians, who tend to forget what people in the real world really care about. Of course, if you want to look at it another way, this is a "limitation" of qualitative research, because we have only the self-report of a limited number of participants. But this is a tremendously liberating revelation to the report writer. Once we realize that our first (not necessarily our most important, but our first) duty is to report what we've heard from a limited number of participants, we have confined the report to a very manageable scope.

In academia, it's sometimes almost impossible to write anything, because we have a nagging feeling that there's one more article we should have read or one more source we should have checked. Not so with reports of qualitative research. Once the groups or one-on-ones are over, they're over. We have a finite amount of data to work with. We report those data, and we draw our conclusions and make our recommendations based on that finite amount of data.

This has some very practical applications. For example, if I am asked to write a full report, I simply organize my Detailed Summary of Findings according to the subheadings of the moderator's guide. My clients always sign off on the guide so I assume my basic responsibilities are

1. to find out what my participants think and feel about those issues outlined in the guide, and
2. to report what they said.

Using the guide as a scaffold for the report doesn't always make for the most creative writing, but it is very efficient and easy to read, and it certainly avoids writer's block. I always know what I have to cover next.

Now, some people will object that simply reporting what we've heard reduces the qualitative researcher to the position of a mere scribe. In fact, Pat Sabena, current president of the Qualitative Research Consultants Association (QRCA), has recently made a point of arguing that European moderators see American moderators as "merely reporters." I am sensitive to that criticism, and that is why I said our *first*, not our most *important* duty is to report what was said. I believe our most important duty is to analyze what we've heard, draw conclusions, and make recommendations. That's what I try to do in the Executive Summary of Findings, which, by the way, I find increasingly is all clients want.

But here, too, we come back to the liberating aspects of the limitations of our endeavor: All of our analysis, conclusions, and recommendations need to be based on whatever our participants said in the two, four, or even a dozen groups under discussion. Even if it is a big project, the data are finite, and that's what we have to work with.

As qualitative researchers, we bring to bear on that analysis years of experience in many different fields—marketing, advertising, sociology, applied linguistics, and others. We have every right to apply what we know to the analysis of what we've heard, but, again, I'd argue that we have to apply it to what we've heard. If, for example, a moderator with a background in advertising has heard that a campaign isn't working, and the participants have suggested why it isn't working and what might work, that moderator can and should make recommendations based on what participants said. However, if that moderator wants to suggest a totally different campaign, based on nothing that he or she has heard in the groups, I would say that doesn't belong in this particular report. If such moderators also want to act as advertising consultants, then more power to them. But that shouldn't be confused with qualitative research.

This realization, too, I think, has a liberating effect on the report writer: We don't have to face every imaginable possibility. We deal with what is in front of us. We examine what we've heard, draw conclusions, and make recommendations based partially on our own years of experience

Finally, that process does not need to be lengthy. As I've tried to insist, the data are limited and finite, and whatever experience we already have is already internalized. So, the analysis is generally an intuitive one. It has to be, because qualitative market research is inductive. We don't have numbers to play with, rearrange, cross-tabulate, and put through extensive analysis. We search the data we have for insights, and insights can come with the speed of light.

An Analysis Strategy Based on Post-Session Debriefings
by David L. Morgan

This is a simplified analysis strategy that basically consists of tape recording carefully formatted debriefing sessions following each focus group. Its chief advantages are its relative low cost and quick turnaround time. It is most useful for smaller projects involving four or five groups and an oral or brief written report. In addition, it works best for projects that use the same set of well-defined questions across all the groups. The main thing that it requires is a reasonably sharp assistant.

Prior to Analysis

Before the first group, the assistant and the moderator need to agree on the assistant's observational goals—that is, what to watch for during the group. In addition, the assistant needs a consistent means for recording these observations. For assistants who do not have prior experience with this analysis strategy, I create a structured data recording sheet that is based on the interview guide. More experienced assistants can record their observations on a version of the interview guide that has lots of "white space" after every question. Either way, the key data to be captured are notes about which topics generated the most energy in the discussion and the extent to which a topic generated either consensus or differences of opinion. The assistant records this information for each question in the interview guide, along with any interesting quotations from that segment of the discussion.

The Debriefing Session

Immediately after each group, the moderator and assistant debrief together using a tape recorder to capture their thoughts. We begin by generating a thumbnail description of the group that includes information on how many participants there were, the group's composition, and any notable circumstances that influenced their discussion. After we discuss and decide on these issues, we turn on the tape recorder and the moderator dictates the thumbnail description. We then turn off the tape recorder and move on the first question. Using the assistant's notes, we go over the major points that came up in the discussion of this question. Once we decide what we should say to summarize this part of the group discussion, the moderator turns the tape back on and dictates this summary. This debriefing proceeds through each question in the guide, following the same process by first discussing and deciding what to say, then dictating a summary of what the group said. After we work our way through the whole guide, we conclude by deciding what were the major themes and most notable points in this group, and then dictate that information.

Writing the Report

I have each debriefing tape transcribed and word processed immediately. Since such a tape typically contains 20 to 30 minutes of dictation, it should take less than an hour to transcribe. If the turnaround time for the project is really tight, I reserve the transcript typist's time in advance, so that the tape can be delivered and picked up according to schedule. To assemble the actual report, I bring all of the debriefing files together in a word processor. If the report requires a group-by-group summary, I recast each transcript as a "top-line" report for that group. I then go over the full set of debriefing summaries to determine what were the key themes across the full set of discussions, as well as how similar the groups were to one another.

I usually begin a brief report by stating the major themes that apply across the full set of groups. If there were important differences across the groups, I describe them here. Then, I go through the rest of the report, question by question from the interview guide. For the write-up of each specific question, I first relate the discussion of that question to the big themes that I stated at the beginning of the report. Then, I summarize additional topics that came up in the discussion of that specific question.

I conclude a report like this with either recommendations or a less forceful statement of my own observations if the research's sponsor did not specifically request recommendations.

See Chapter 11
For More
Information on
Top-Line Reports

Computerized Analysis
by David L. Morgan

My work often calls for me to analyze focus group data for publication in refereed, academic journals. I call the approach I use "qualitative content analysis," and I've described various aspects of it in a series of publications that I did from my research on caregiving for family members with Alzheimer's disease. This was a large project (35 focus groups), so I conducted the analyses using the computer. In addition, analyzing large data sets often means working with a research team, and that was definitely the case in the project I will describe here. Although I supervised and participated in every phase of the analysis, five research assistants did the bulk of the coding.

For this summary of my analysis process, I want to emphasize the role that the computer plays. What I describe below is based on using The Ethnograph, but working with other software packages would be similar. For those who are not familiar with using qualitative analysis software, it is important to clarify just what the computer does and does not do. First of all, it doesn't "do the analysis." I find it more useful to think of the computer as a powerful indexing and cross-referencing tool. As you locate segments of the data that you want to label or "code," the program records your analytic efforts; later, it allows you to search for and retrieve these codes, just as a good index in a book would. Still, it is up to you to figure out not only what set of coding categories to use but also where to apply each code in the text you are analyzing. In other words, you do the analysis, and the computer records and systematizes your work. Using a computer is no substitute for reading and thinking about the data!

During the Group

To record the data in the most useful fashion, it is necessary to keep track of who said what during the group. The easiest way to do this is to have the assistant keep a "speaker log." We give each participant an ID number at the start and then keep a running record of the first phrase or so of what each speaker says. For example:

#3 The hardest part for us was . . .

#6 We never had that . . .

During the transcription process, the typist both listens to the tape and follows through the log, inserting the proper ID number at the start of what each participant says. The transcript thus contains clear data about who said what. The obvious advantage of this system is that it makes it easy to tell if the whole group has an interest in a topic or if just one person mentioned it repeatedly.

You may also want to include data that the software will attach to either individual speakers or the group as a whole. This may be from the observer's note taking or from variables in a questionnaire. For example, in our work with Alzheimer's caregivers, the assistant noted each participant's gender. Using this information in the software allowed us to do separate searches to list the codes from statements by male and female caregivers.

To move from the tape recordings to the computer involves transcribing the data in a word-processing program according to the analysis software's required format. This is usually not difficult for a trained typist, but it does take some careful planning and checking. When working with new typists, we usually have them do a small trial section of a transcript and check that, rather than having to reformat a whole transcript that didn't match what the software required.

Codebooks Are Central to the Analysis Process

In order to mark and retrieve sections of text, you need a set of codes that capture your key analytic constructs. For example, in the Alzheimer's caregiving research, we used two basic types of codes. The first type captured social network data by marking all references to other people, using code categories such as spouse, neighbor, or doctor. The second type of code captured the different types of stresses associated with caregiving, including problems with time, money, exhaustion, emotions, lack of information, and family conflict.

I usually plan to make at least two coding "passes" through the transcripts. In between the two passes, our research team updates and refines our initial codebook, based on what we learned in our first pass through the data. We thus start with a simpler set of codes and expand it as we become more familiar with the data.

The first pass involves reading the entire text of each transcript to apply the initial set of codes. I usually begin with relatively simple sets of codes that can be easily applied to the data as soon as they arrive. This first pass thus makes heavy use of so-called manifest content codes, which are concrete things that can immediately be recognized and marked. In the Alzheimer's study, we used more than 20 manifest content codes for relationship categories: father, mother, sister, brother, and so on.

For more complex, and thus less "manifest," codes, I prefer to start with broad categories in the first-pass coding. For example, among our initial stress categories, we knew that emotions would be a very complex area, but we wanted to let our coding of emotional issues emerge from the data. To do that, we began by finding as many instances of emotional stresses as we could during the first-pass coding.

The second coding pass through the data essentially refines and updates the code categories from the first pass. On the one hand, it cleans up manifest content categories if there were some items that we had not anticipated in the initial coding system. More critically, it expands and refines the coding system for initially broad codes into more specific categories. For example, an earlier broad code category such as emotional stress would become several well-specified subcategories.

How the Software Makes a Difference

The main thing that using a computer does is to make your analytic efforts very systematic. It forces you to think through what you are doing, prior to proceeding with each step, and it provides a formalized record of what you do. This is especially useful if your work is likely to be "audited" or otherwise reviewed by others. The computerized record, as embodied in codebooks and codes applied to transcript segments, makes any inconsistencies in the analytic process all too obvious.

and codes applied to transcript segments, makes any inconsistencies in the analytic process all too obvious.

Using computer software also makes it much easier to update and modify your coding systems. This is especially useful in a two-pass coding system, because you can search out instances of specific codes that need to be expanded or updated. Thus, rather than having to reread all the text in every transcript to recode specific forms of emotional stress, the computer can locate every instance of the initial broad code category, so that the analyst can read each passage and assign the appropriate additional code(s) to it.

Using the computer to locate coded sections of the transcript is called searching, and this is one of the most powerful advantages in using a software package. The most obvious thing you can do is to find and list all instances of a particular code. For example, suppose you want to examine all the instances of a broad, first-pass code category, so that you can begin to create a more refined set of subcategories for a second pass. It would take only a single command to search through all of the transcripts at once, collect the appropriately coded material into a new file, and print it all out, along with information about from which group and speaker(s) each passage came. The computer also makes it possible to do more complex searches using the Boolean operators AND, OR, and NOT. For example, we could search for all instances of emotional problems that also involve family conflict, and we could further refine the results of this search to separate out instances that include siblings but not other family members —and so on.

To Count or Not to Count

One of the options that goes along with searching is counting. In the example about family conflict, combining searching and counting would make it easy to state the percentage of the instances of family conflict that involved siblings. In the caregiving study, we used Boolean searching to compose tables of counts, including one that compared the number of positive versus negative things that caregivers said about primary-care physicians versus specialists.

Such counting is not for everyone, but I use it for a specific purpose. My goal is to use counts to detect patterns in the data. If I want to compare what family caregivers say about using primary-care physicians versus specialists, it helps to know that they are much more likely to mention negative things about primary-care physicians. The advantage of this approach is that it reduces speculation. Within the limits of the coding system, I

I do not, however, stop my analysis once I have these descriptive numbers. Instead, I take the patterns that I detect as the starting point for a more reflective interpretation of why these patterns occur. This means asking questions like: If siblings provoke the majority of family conflicts, how does this occur? Or, if primary-care doctors are viewed so negatively, why is this so? Answering these kinds of question inevitably involves going back in and reading the transcripts again. Of course, the searching capacities of computer can help you locate what you want to read, but they do not provide any insight about the kinds of "how" and "why" questions that are at the heart of qualitative analysis. This is why I call the kind of content analysis that I do "qualitative content analysis." Using computerized coding to describe the content in the data is just the beginning of the larger qualitative process of interpretation.

Do You Really Need to Use the Computer?

Most of what I have described here is a logical process, consisting of steps like creating codebooks, applying them in two (or more) passes, separating out descriptive counting from interpretive reading, and so on. None of this really requires a computer, but it would be hard to do by hand if you had more than a few groups. I personally would judge six groups to be near the upper limit for doing this kind of systematic coding with colored pencils, highlighting pens, marginal notes, and the like. I don't mean that you couldn't do more than six groups by hand, but at that point the computer not only saves a great deal of time but also ensures that the work is done in a thorough and consistent fashion.

The real question, however, is not whether you want to use a computer, but whether you want to be this systematic. What is the purpose for doing such a thorough and detailed analysis? Most often, this is an audience issue: Who will you be responsible to and in what ways? If the analysis will be the basis for an article to be reviewed at an academic journal, then this kind of systematic effort may well be essential. Similarly, graduate students must be able to show their thesis committees exactly how they reached their conclusions. It might also be important to have the kind of record that a computerized analysis generates if you are working on a major grant, especially when there will be an outside audit or other assessment of your work. This style of analysis is a way of life for some of us, but for the vast majority of applied focus group projects in organizations and agencies, the procedures described here would amount to pointless "overkill."

Analyzing and Reporting Focus Group Results
by Marilyn J. Rausch

If you have ever been handed a set of tapes or transcriptions and asked to analyze and write a report for focus groups you did not design or moderate, you may have discovered that the process should start at the very beginning, not near the end of a project. When I explore the study problem and objectives with my client, I am really asking, "What do you want in the report?" When I ascertain how the report will be used and who will read it, I begin to determine how I will write the report—how much depth, what language, which report style. When I bid the project or prepare a cost estimate, I may give clients the option of a summary report or a comprehensive report, and when they state their preferences, I know a lot about how I will be reporting the results.

The question flow or discussion guide can become the framework for your report. If the guide seemed logical during the sessions and if the questions resulted in data that were "on purpose," the report can be written from the guide. I write my guides in classic outline style because these lend themselves well to the process of report writing. The report falls easily into major headings and subheadings. If the "meat" of the session falls at the end of your question flow or discussion guide (as it often does), there may be a need to reorder sections from the most to the least important for the report.

When there are multiple sessions, you need to decide whether you will analyze vertically or horizontally. I decide what makes sense in terms of the research design and then stick with it throughout the report. For example, if the project consisted of four groups of school nurses talking about issues they face in administering medications to students, the report might best be written horizontally—common issues from across the groups are reported. If the same project comprised one group each of students, parents, school nurses, and principals, then the report might best be written vertically, where the issues voiced by each group are discussed separately, with commonalities addressed at the conclusion.

Not all results have to be reported. Off-the-topic comments are excluded. Nice-to-know data often just pad the report to no purpose. Deciding what to report and what not to report is an art—an art that can only be sharpened by experience. Here are hints to assist in the process of deciding what to report and not report:

- Look for common themes. If every topic discussed ends with "but we don't think it can be done," you have discovered an overall credibility or believability roadblock.
- Look for repeatedly voiced attitudes or opinions, and then try to identify the dissenting opinions. Regardless of the size of the camps, try to describe both sides.
- Be on the alert for the single response that for some reason seems worthy of note, even if it was heard only once. Occasionally, these responses identify a critical problem or a fabulous opportunity that others have not yet recognized.
- Always listen for what you do not hear. A whole discussion about a new product idea in which price is never mentioned until probed represents data that should be reported.
- When in doubt about whether or not to include something, go back to the problem definition and list of objectives and ask, "Does this information contribute to the accomplishment of these objectives?"

Typically, I follow these steps in analysis and report writing:

1. Read through all of the transcriptions, annotating and highlighting key findings and potential quotes.
2. Write a rough draft of the detailed findings.
3. Go back to the transcriptions and select verbatim quotes to illustrate the findings.
4. Reread and edit the draft with the executive summary in mind.
5. Write an executive summary with key findings and recommendations or concluding remarks sections. (This is placed at the beginning of the report.)
6. Append copies of the discussion guide and any other pertinent study material.

9

Advice for
First-Timers

Overview

Few, Few, Few
Keep It Simple
Remember the Purpose and What the Client Wants
Ask Final Questions
Tape and Transcribe Yourself
Work With an Assistant
Work With a Mentor

Your first analysis project will be the hardest. Everything is new, you have no comparative studies, all details look important, and you lack experience. If you're fortunate, you'll have a mentor to provide advice. Here are suggestions we give beginning moderators.

Few, Few, Few

As soon as possible, conduct several focus groups on a topic of interest to you. Our advice is "few, few, few." Do a few groups. Do them with a few people. Do them with a few questions. Sometimes, novice moderators feel they have to do everything "according to the book" the first time. Consequently, they launch into too many focus groups with too many participants and too many questions, and they are overwhelmed. Begin with two or three focus groups. Use these groups as learning opportunities. Within each group, recruit about four or five people and limit the discussion to about five or six questions. These smaller groups are easier to assemble, manage, and analyze. Once you are comfortable with your moderating and analyzing skills, increase the number of groups, participants, and questions.

Keep It Simple

Simplicity is essential, and it occurs in several dimensions. Limit the study to one key theme or concept, instead of branching into several areas of importance. Keep the focus simple by having the questions clearly and logically connect with each other. Smooth segues and natural transitions help participants maintain the line of thought and thereby improve the analysis. The easiest way to bring simplicity into the study is through clear questions. By keeping the questions simple and clear, and then by consistently asking the same questions in each group, the analysis task is easier. Avoid compound sentences. Some focus groups are impossible to analyze because the questions are asked differently in each group or because the questions are ambiguous and the moderator fails to follow up with clarifying questions. A clearly defined purpose and clear questions are the starting point.

Remember the Purpose and What the Client Wants

Don't forget the purpose of the study. This advice is particularly appropriate in nonprofit and public sector focus groups. Clients may be imprecise about what they want, or the study purpose may evolve and creep into different areas. Veteran moderators have experienced this before and are careful about adding time-consuming tasks.

The challenge is to have a firm grasp of the purpose and to know the boundaries of the study. You may decide to broaden the study into additional areas or examine topics that were not anticipated, such as including recommendations when they were not originally specified. If you do, then do so consciously, with an awareness of the additional time required.

Consultants may attempt to go beyond the contract expectations to please the client, and indeed, this practice can result in satisfied clients and contracts. The novice is at a disadvantage because he or she has not had experience with factors that can dramatically increase the time demands. Certainly, confusion over purpose results in a substantial time investment because the analyst is attempting to cover too much territory.

Ask Final Questions

The final questions take on particular importance for the beginning moderator. These questions are crucial to gain a sense of what the participants deem to be important or noteworthy. These questions enable the moderator to get verification of critical concepts, determine where participants place priority, and foster confidence that the appropriate topics were discussed. Moreover, the ending question helps diagnose problems. If something goes wrong, the moderator can ask participants if changes are needed in the questions, the environment, or other factors. The ending question allows the moderator to invite participant suggestions on what went wrong or offer advice on future focus groups.

For More Information About Ending Question See Chapter 4 of *Developing Questions for Focus Groups*

Tape and Transcribe Yourself

One of the most meaningful learning opportunities comes from listening and transcribing the tape from your focus group. Without question, this is time-consuming, and you should expect to spend about two days preparing the transcription. If at all possible, attempt to prepare the transcript yourself for the first few focus groups. This process, tedious as it may be, accomplishes two purposes: first, it improves moderating, and second, it improves analysis.

Self-transcribing improves moderating because typing everything that you said will cause you to agonize as to why you talked so much on some questions and then failed to probe or follow up on other topics. Generally, novice moderators talk too quickly and too often. Veterans have discovered the power of pauses. By waiting for comments, valuable answers can emerge.

Self-transcribing improves analysis because it helps the novice moderator become intimately connected with the data. You become immersed in the comments because you've now experienced each comment several times. By looking back over the discussion and replaying it several times, the moderator can find the threads of the discussion and determine how comments are connected, when the discussion gets off track, and how the moderator functions to maintain control. In transcribing, you are looking for notable quotes, and after listening, typing, and read-ing, you are very familiar with the discussion. Some statements leap out as being helpful in analysis. Interestingly, you may not have spotted these during the discussion, but now, because you've pondered over the comments several times, the distinction is clearer. This exercise of spotting notable quotes is valuable in moderating and analyzing future focus groups because it helps the researcher quickly identify those quotes that might appear in the final report.

Work With an Assistant

For an Overview of the Assistant Moderator Role, Look Over Chapter 10 of *Moderating Focus Groups*

Have someone help you during the focus groups. This helper knows about the study, focus groups, and you. Review the potential responsibilities of the assistant moderator and decide how they will be handled.

The assistant provides you with moral support and encour-agement. Moreover, this person helps with the arrangements, capturing of information, and analysis. The challenge for novice analysts is to know how much attention to place on themes, to decide whether or not an emerging topic is worthy of further discussion and analysis, and to balance the demands of logistics and of paying attention to participants. The second person becomes your copilot, your coach, and your confidant.

Work With a Mentor

The most meaningful help will likely be from a mentor. As discussed in the previous point, an assistant can help you. If at all possible, locate an assistant with focus group experience. For years, beginning focus group moderators learned their skills by apprenticing with master moderators. If possible, watch a master conduct focus groups. In the first few focus groups, you might serve as the assistant moderator and then switch places with the master. This not only provides you with helpful advice on the moderating, but it also enhances your analysis. After the focus group, debrief with the master and listen to his or her com-ments and observations. After a few groups, you might lead the debriefing discussion, with your mentor providing you with a critique.

It's hard to find a mentor. Do your homework, and be deliberate in your quest. Often, you'll get further if you are referred by a mutual friend, colleague, or associate. Because moderators tend to specialize in topic areas, consider the area you wish to develop. Find out who the expert moderators are in that topic area in your community. Assume that the potential mentor is not looking for additional help. What can you do or offer that will be of benefit to the potential mentor? You are asking for a sizable investment of time and little or no payoff for the mentor. How can you make yourself appealing? Are you willing to work for little or no pay in order to develop skills? Are you willing to volunteer to do other tasks in the organization or firm that will help the mentor if he or she will work with you? One of the most successful strategies for finding a mentor is for your organization to hire an expert to conduct the study and to write into the contract that the expert serves as a mentor to a select number of employees. Just remember, it won't be easy to find a mentor, but if you do, it will be worth the effort.

TIP

Finding a Mentor

Part III

Sharing Results

Question: What is truer than the truth?
Answer: The story.

(Old Jewish saying)

In Part III, we will share how to tell the story of the results. Of all the parts of the focus group study, reporting is perhaps most overlooked and neglected task. Indeed, we often assume that our traditional ways of doing things are good enough. However, with a little effort and thought, the benefit can be enormous. Public and nonprofit organizations have special challenges and opportunities that do not occur in private-sector focus group studies, such as the need for widespread distribution, the influence of public opinion, and the potential benefits of volunteers. We shall explore these and also review strategies for written and oral reporting.

Throughout this part, there are five principles at the foundation of reporting. Later, we'll refer to these in various ways, but here, we'll be very explicit. These are the five principles:

Know the Point and Get to It Quickly

No matter what type of report—written or spoken, formal or informal, one-to-one or to a large group—always know the point and get to it quickly. Everything in the report has a purpose.

Clear, Effective Writing Takes Time

Short reports will take longer to prepare. In 1657, Blaise Pascal wrote, "I have made this letter longer than usual, only because I have not had the time to make it shorter."

Provide Enlightenment

Some reports reinforce existing views or opinions, but the primary purpose is to enlighten someone—to bring knowledge, provide understanding, and convey information. Ask yourself, "What do I have that is new, important, and valuable to my audience?" Too often, reporters feel their role is to impress, to convey the rigor of the study, or to carry some other message. The best reporters know the point, present it quickly, and select that point because it provides enlightenment.

Involve Other People Throughout the Study

In the public and nonprofit environment, focus groups that involve other people throughout the study tend to produce better results. People can be involved in planning, recruiting, moderating, analyzing, or reporting aspects of the focus group study. When people are involved, the results tend to be used. A group of other people involved in sharing focus group results multiplies the potential in several respects.

Use Multiple Reporting Strategies

People have preferred learning styles. We need reinforcement and reminders. We access information in different ways. Successful reporting uses multiple methods, such as one-to-one, oral briefings, reports, presentations, media, and so on.

10

Principles of Reporting

Overview

Remember the Purpose of the Study
Consider the Audience
Consider the Options

Remember the Purpose of the Study

Occasionally, we forget why we are reporting. In many instances, reporting serves a practical, functional purpose, such as conveying information to decision makers about perceptions. In other situations, the purpose might be for academic research or the discovery or confirmation of theory. At times, the report serves as a signal to funders that the grantee is conscientious and attentive to discovery and improvement. The report may also serve as a signal that the grantee is documenting accountability for the resources provided. Confusion can result when we operate with multiple purposes or when we are not clear as to why the study was conducted. Therefore, the first principle is to be crystal clear about the purpose of reporting and the intended audience.

The process of reporting serves three functions. First and foremost, reports communicate results. The underlying principle of reporting is that the report communicates useful information to an identifiable audience for a specific purpose. For this communication to be effective, the reporter must select the appropriate media, strive for clarity and precision of expression, and pay attention to the individual information needs of specific people. The report can assist decision makers, announce research results, help community residents understand local needs, or a host of other purposes.

Second, the process of preparing reports assists the researcher in developing a logical description of the investigation. This function takes place during the preparation of reports, particularly the written report. Report writing is a disciplined effort that helps the researcher arrange the findings, conclusions, and recommendations in a logical sequence that can be subjected to review. This disciplined effort results in tighter logic, more precise statements, and an overall improvement in quality.

The process of reporting also produces a written report that is a historical record of the study. While a written report is intended primarily to serve more immediate needs of audiences, it also can provide a longer term reference for future studies and decisions. Concerns and problems often reemerge. The environment may change, the original recommendations for improving the program may not work, and decision makers may need to reexamine or even replicate earlier studies. Therefore, one of the purposes of the report is to provide a document that can be subjected to examination at some point in the future.

Consider the Audience

The researcher begins reporting efforts by reflecting on the audience—those who will be receiving and using the report. A problem in reporting is fuzzy identification of the audience. Researchers have a tendency to prepare reports for amorphous groups—the organization, the feds, the board—as opposed to specific people. A helpful strategy is to reflect on the identified users and assemble information of particular interest to these individuals. In some situations, different reports can be prepared for different audiences, with each report emphasizing areas of concern and interest to each user category.

Those who prepare reports tend to assume that people prefer to learn about results in the same way that the researcher prefers. This assumption is in conflict with what is known about individual learning preferences. Evidence suggests that people differ on how they prefer to receive information. This leads us to two implications for researchers. First, they should learn as much as they can about their audiences' preferences in receiving information. Educational level, occupation, age, and other demographic data can be helpful in this inquiry.

Second, researchers need to use a variety of media. Reports can be prepared for presentation in several ways: in writing, orally, or complemented with visuals, charts, photographs, audiotapes and videotapes, tables, or figures, just to name some of the options. Procedures used are limited only by resources and creativity. Reports using multiple media help ensure that the message is effectively communicated because the combination of methods accommodates individual learning preferences and also provides reinforcement of the findings.

Consider the Options

Focus group reports can be of three types: oral only, written only, or a combination of both oral and written. Whenever possible, the researcher should attempt to provide the report in a combination of modes, because each method offers unique advantages. Oral reports allow for questions, clarification, and the use of taped highlights or quotations. Written reports are well suited for distribution within an organization, and they are essential when it is difficult to gather people together. When oral and written reports are used together, the advantages are multiplied.

When preparing written reports, the emphasis is on clarity and understanding. The writing style is characterized by less formality, shorter words, and a familiar vocabulary. Use the active rather than the passive voice. Use of quotations, illustrations, or examples of concepts is encouraged. When writing for nonresearchers, the complex descriptions of analysis and technical jargon actually inhibit understanding. Complex research procedures, if used, must be explained in an understandable way to those not acquainted with them.

11

Written Reports

Overview

Narrative Report
Report Memo
Top-Line Report
Bulleted Report

Focus group reports have traditionally been presented in a narrative style. Alternatives include the report memo, the top-line report, and the bulleted report. Let's review the key ingredients of each of these. Because the narrative report is the most traditional, we'll examine it first.

Narrative Report

The narrative report is recognized by its length and its use of quotations. Typically, these reports are somewhere between 10 and 30 pages long, but occasionally, a report might become lengthy, reaching close to 100 pages. The danger of excessive length is that it limits readability, except for the most interested and ardent client.

Besides being clear and logical, the written report must also look attractive. Poor-quality printing, inadequate covers, and shoddy assembly convey undesirable impressions of the total research effort. If necessary, the researcher should seek assistance in editing the report for clarity, misspellings, and grammatical mistakes.

BACKGROUND

**Outline for
Written Report**

1. *Cover Page.* *The front cover should include the title, names of people receiving or commissioning the report, the names of the researchers, and the date the report is submitted.*

2. *Summary.* *The brief, well-written executive summary describes why the focus groups were conducted and lists the major findings and recommendations. The summary is often limited to two pages and should be able to stand alone. Although this section is placed first in the written report, it is often the last part written.*

3. *Table of Contents.* *This section is optional and need not be included when the report is brief. The table of contents provides the reader with information on how the report is organized and where various parts are located.*

4. *Purpose and Procedures.* *In this section, the researcher should describe the purpose of the study and include a brief description of the focus group interviews. Remember your audience. Academics may want a detailed description of procedures, but most readers aren't interested in much beyond the number of groups, types of people included as participants, and where the groups were held. Often, it is helpful to describe in general terms the thought process behind the question route. The questions are not included here but may be included in the appendix. Sometimes, the discussion of procedures or methods is moved to the appendix.*

5. *Results or Findings.* *Most often, results are organized around key questions, themes, or big ideas. The decision on how to arrange your findings should be based on the purpose of the study. The conventional style is to take the questions in sequence. The limitation is that this style begins with the least important information, for indeed, the critical questions and more valuable results occur later in the focus group. In addition, some of the information is redundant because the same themes appear in several questions. Therefore, consider organizing by themes and begin with those points that are most beneficial to the reader.*

6. *Summary or Conclusions.* *A limited number of themes or key points are cited here. These statements are not limited to specific questions but often tie together themes that bridge several questions, if not the entire discussion. In this section, the researcher discusses factors or threads that cut across specific points. Occasionally, the researcher will draw attention to a finding that was unanticipated but nevertheless important to the study.*

7. *Recommendations.* *Recommendations are optional and not automatically included in focus group reports. The recommendations are future-oriented and provide suggestions as to what might be done with the results. Sometimes, they are expressed in very specific terms, and in other circumstances, they are more generally stated. This section is sometimes presented as "suggestions" or "ideas to consider" or other words that convey less formality.*

8. *Appendix.* *The final part of the written report is the appendix, which includes additional materials that might be helpful to the reader. For example, it is advisable to include the questioning route and the screening questionnaire. Additional quotations may also be included in the appendix. In some situations, the author may wish to include limitations and alternative interpretations.*

Perhaps the most challenging aspect of the written report is the preparation of recommendations. The ability to do this well is what some people say distinguishes "data collectors" from "valuable consultants." Consultants have the ability to see implications and recommend action that results in successful changes. Recommendations are challenging because they go beyond the evidence from the study to include other insights about the environment—traditions, barriers, and context of the organization and the problem. Therefore, it is valuable to have others assist the research team in preparing these recommendations. Decision makers may see the need for an entirely different course of action, and discussion is needed to arrive at the most desirable course of action. For example, in a recent university study, an important finding was the discovery of low faculty morale. The research team assumed that clear administrative changes were needed to address inequalities, remove barriers, and change incentives. When administrators read the report, their recommendation was that faculty should just quit whining.

A basic decision made by the analyst is what to include in the narrative report. The skeleton or framework of the report is typically composed of the key questions or the big ideas that have emerged from the discussion. These questions and big ideas serve as the outline for the results or findings section. These results can be presented using three different styles or models. The first style of presentation consists of the question or idea, followed by participant comments (the raw data model). The second style is a summary description, followed by illustrative quotes (the descriptive model). The third style is a summary description with illustrative quotes, followed by an interpretation (the interpretive model).

Here are examples of these styles from a series of focus group interviews with parents. The first example illustrates the reporting of raw data. In this example, the researcher included comments arranged into clusters or categories. The categories were selected by the researcher after reviewing all comments.

When appropriate, the comments can be arranged on a continuum, such as degree of support, agreement versus disagreement, intensity, and so on. This style of reporting has the advantage of providing the reader with a range of comments; however, the sheer length of the resulting report discourages careful reading. The raw data model of reporting is particularly appropriate when you are summarizing one focus group, when the researcher has limited experience (when volunteers conduct the focus groups), when the sponsor is interested in receiving a sizable number of comments, or when a descriptive or interpretive report follows.

EXAMPLE

Raw Data

Q. What do you look for in a youth organization?

Responses from parents included:

Category 1: Quality of Leaders

Good leaders who can be a role model. (J., May 2)

The person in charge must be a good influence because children idolize their leaders. (M., May 2)

I would like my son in a youth organization that has a dedicated adult leader. My son needs to succeed in something other than school. I want him to have the feeling of accomplishment that comes with hard work. (B., May 2)

Leaders are the most important thing in a youth organization. I don't want a crank for a leader. (E., May 2)

I want an adult who is patient and kind to work with my kids. (G., May 3)

Good leaders can accept kids just as they are. These adults can have fun with kids. They can laugh with kids and enjoy the company of young people. (S., May 3)

When I drop my daughter off at the youth organization for the first time, I watch what she does. If the leader brings her into the group and makes her feel welcome, I know that is a good leader. (R., May 3)

I was in scouts when I was young, and I still remember my scoutmaster. He had a sense of humor and always brought out the best in all of us. He always had time to listen to our problems. (B., May 3)

Category 2: Fits with Lifestyle: Cost or Convenience

Low cost. I can't afford uniforms and costly trips. (B., May 2)

I've got four kids, and I'm not going to run them to four different organizations. Either all the kids get involved in one organization, or none at all. (T., May 3)

Any organization that we would consider must be convenient. We have certain family times, and the group can't interfere with that. (E., May 2)

Both my wife and I work. We just don't have time to run both Jim and Jessica, our two kids, to different organizations. The youth organization has to be close enough so that our kids can walk. (B., May 3)

Distance from our home. The organization needs to be within walking or biking distance of our house. (G., May 3)

Cost is somewhat of a factor. (R., May 3)

Category 3: Emphasis of the Youth Organization

You know, what is most important for me is to be certain that the other parents are like me. I mean, we must have the same values on things like drinking and drugs. (J., May 2)

A wholesome environment. I want my son to be around the good kids in the community. (B., May 2)

A chance to get exercise and be out-of-doors. (M., May 2)

My son needs to be in a group setting. He has trouble getting along with others and needs to learn to cooperate and compromise. (G., May 3)

The only group activity my children need is the church. Everything they need is within the church. (S., May 2)

My daughter needs to be able to do something she can feel good about and to have the opportunity to do well. She's not sports-minded and needs an opportunity to get recognition for her own talents. (R., May 3)

Lots of activities. I want my kid to be busy. You know what they say about idle hands. (T., May 3)

The next example is a descriptive summary. This style of reporting begins with a summary paragraph and then includes illustrative quotes. The quotes selected are intended to help the reader understand the way in which respondents answered the question.

EXAMPLE

Descriptive Summary

Q. What do you as a parent look for in a youth organization?

Parents most often cited two characteristics: quality of adult leadership and how the organization fits with the family lifestyle. Parents want their children exposed to adults who understand and relate well to youth. The issue of quality leadership was expressed in different ways, with more attention placed on personal attributes than on the knowledge or technical expertise of the volunteer. In this community, parents are also very concerned that youth organizations not get in the way of family, employment, or other social commitments. Parents favored youth organizations that fit with their present lifestyle. Factors mentioned with lesser frequency related to the emphasis of the youth organization and the opportunity for youth to achieve.

Typical comments by these parents included:

The person in charge must be a good influence because children idolize their leaders. (M., May 2)

Leaders are the most important thing in a youth organization. I don't want a crank for a leader. (E., May 2)

I want an adult who is patient and kind to work with my kids. (G., May 3)

Low cost. I can't afford uniforms and costly trips. (B., May 2)

I've got four kids, and I'm not going to run them to four different organizations. Either all the kids get involved in one organization, or none at all. (T., May 3)

Any organization that we would consider must be convenient. We have certain family times, and the group can't interfere with that. (E., May 2)

The interpretive report builds on the descriptive report by including a section on what the data mean.

EXAMPLE

Interpretive Summary

Q. What do you as a parent look for in a youth organization?

In each group session, the parents cited a number of factors with two characteristics mentioned most often. These were the quality of adult leadership and the importance of convenience. Parents were concerned that their children be exposed to adults who understood and related well to youth. The issue of quality leadership was expressed in different ways, with attention placed more on personal attributes rather than on the knowledge or technical expertise of the volunteer. In this community, the parents were also very concerned about youth organizations not getting in the way of family, employment, or other social commitments. Parents favored youth organizations that were convenient, given their present lifestyle. Factors mentioned with lesser frequency related to the emphasis of the youth organization and the opportunity for youth to achieve.

Typical comments by these parents included:

> The person in charge must be a good influence because children idolize their leaders. (M., May 2)

> Leaders are the most important thing in a youth organization. I don't want a crank for a leader. (E., May 2)

> I want an adult who is patient and kind to work with my kids. (G., May 3)

> Low cost. I can't afford uniforms and costly trips. (B., May 2)

> I've got four kids, and I'm not going to run them to four different organizations. Either all the kids get involved in one organization, or none at all. (T., May 3)

> Any organization that we would consider must be convenient. We have certain family times, and the group can't interfere with that. (E., May 2)

Some parents had a strong sense of family values and recognized that participation in youth organizations can support those values (through caring leaders with similar values) or erode them (by taking time away from family activities). Other parents were tired from their hectic work schedules. They don't want anything that makes an already overloaded life more difficult.

The raw data reporting style is faster and easier for the researcher, but this style essentially transfers the work of analysis to the readers of the report. This style is recommended only as a prelude to the descriptive or interpretive styles or in situations where the analyst has limited skills or the audience prefers reviewing a sizable number of relevant comments. Both the descriptive and interpretive styles have the advantage of data reduction, with the interpretive procedure providing the greatest depth in analysis.

Report Memo

The report memo is a brief summary of key findings that typically is one or two pages in length. This report is usually written by the sponsor, with help from the analyst, and sent to people who participated in the series of focus groups. The purpose is to assure participants that they were heard by highlighting the key findings and the response by the sponsor. This report often goes beyond the findings to identify recommendations or suggestions for action. In some cases, it also identifies progress toward these goals. Often, this report is used in concert with a longer narrative report that might reference this document. The information in the memo is personalized to a particular audience, and more than one memo may be prepared from the same report, each one emphasizing items of concern for a particular group.

In the public and nonprofit sectors, the report memo can be sent to focus group participants and others interested in the study results. Focus groups in the public and nonprofit environments are dramatically different from private sector focus groups because public sector results are often shared widely with members, customers, patrons, or elected officials, whereas the private sector tends to have greater concern about proprietary information. Often, focus group participants in the public sector want to see the results of the listening process, especially if there was considerable participant energy involved in the focus group discussions. If no results are evident, there is a tendency for the participants to assume that the organization is nonresponsive. For example, in some communities of color and in some organizations, people have expressed hesitancy to participate in focus groups because they haven't seen results from past listening.

An effective strategy is to include four items in the report memo. First, the memo thanks participants for sharing their ideas and taking the time to participate. Second, the memo contains a summary of key findings. Third, the recommendations that resulted from the findings are described. Finally, there is a description of what is now being done, or what will be done, to accomplish the recommendations.

The following report was prepared for the Chair of the Department of Rhetoric at the University of Minnesota and for a planning committee for the annual Institute for Technical Communication (ITC). In previous years, the Institute had been offered for academics. The committee wanted to change the focus and design a program that would interest practicing technical communicators as well as academics. Thus, they commissioned a small market study of technical communicators from the Minneapolis-St. Paul area to gather information about their continuing education practices and needs.

EXAMPLE

Report Memo

MEMORANDUM

To: *ITC Planning Committee*

From: *Sandra Becker*

Re: *Focus Group Report*

As you requested, I have completed two group interviews of technical communicators from the Twin Cities area. Using the membership list of the Twin Cities' Society for Technical Communicators, I invited an equal mix of managers and non-managers as well as corporate and contract writers drawn at random. The uniformity of responses between the two groups seems to indicate that the results of the interviews are reasonably reliable.

The following information provided by the groups should help you make decisions about the program, pricing, and promotional tactics for next year's ITC. Based on those findings, I offer several recommendations for your consideration.

Findings

1. *Employers sponsored outside training opportunities for all respondents. Companies paid up to $200/day for courses that lasted up to three days. All of the courses were technical in nature.*
2. *Courses longer than three days would not be well received by employers.*
3. *Sponsorship and credibility of instructors, the topics of training, timing, and location were the most important factors considered by potential participants. No single factor seemed more important than others.*
4. *The following topics, in descending order of importance, were suggested as areas where employers weren't providing adequate training:*
   a. *On-line documentation*
   b. *Company politics, especially the role of the writer on the design team and within the company*
   c. *Project management, i.e., scheduling, estimating, budgeting*
   d. *Design, graphics, and graphics production*
   e. *Product evaluation*
   f. *The writer as teacher*
   g. *Product liability and the technical writer*

Recommendations

1. *Keep the Institute less than four days. One of those days (or at least a half-day) could fall on a Saturday to demonstrate to employers the seriousness of the writers' desire to participate in the program. Keep the Institute in July as you have in the past.*
2. *Charge over $100/day, since the market will bear a $200/day fee if the topics are of interest to potential participants.*
3. *Since both groups concurred about the topics listed above, I think you should incorporate as many of their suggestions as possible into the program.*

4. *Use their language in your promotional materials. For example, instead of listing instructional design as a topic, use their phrase, the writer as teacher or simply teaching.*
5. *Stress that the University is sponsoring the Institute and include some well-known experts on the program, since sponsorship and the expertise of presenters are considered important.*

I would be happy to meet with your program subcommittee to provide additional information about the topics suggested by the respondents.

The following report memo was sent to focus group participants following a national series of focus groups on customer service. Note that the letter describes actions already taken and actions anticipated.

EXAMPLE

**Report Memo
Cover Letter**

United States Department of Agriculture
National Food and Agriculture Council

Name

Address

City, State, Zip

Thank you for having taken time from your busy schedule to do us the favor of participating in one of the USDA focus groups we held this past winter. We knew of no better way to ensure that our USDA Service Centers will truly serve you than to ask you about your experiences, opinions and needs. That was our goal with these focus groups. You came, you talked, and I assure you we have been listening.

I read the enclosed report very carefully and have shared it with Secretary Glickman and the key management team in USDA. They, like I, are struck by your honesty, frankness and commitment to helping us improve our service to you. We have begun to act on what you told us. Here are some of the things we have already done.

We have developed and published customer service standards, reflecting what you told us. These standards are part of the enclosed USDA Service Center brochure. Copies are being sent to every USDA Service Center around the country. To make sure we deliver on those standards, the Secretary wants to make sure all our employees who work directly with the public are familiar with these customer service standards and how to achieve them. The Secretary also wants an easy-to-use, responsive, feedback and complaint system to be available to our customers.

Between now and the first of October 1996 we are pilot testing a training course for our employees who work directly with the public. Our goal is to do more than just meet your expectations of us. We want to exceed your expectations. You and all our customers deserve nothing less than the finest service which can be provided. We have also been testing a process where a sample of customers receive a telephone call shortly after they do business with us. The purpose of this call is to learn what we are doing well and what we can improve. We have contacted other customers by mail to learn more about how we are doing. We will probably conduct some more focus groups on selected customer service topics. Finally, I have also directed a small group to look at developing a feedback and complaint system which will be, as you suggested, easy-to-use, prompt and responsive. I want a complaint system to be in-place soon—before Thanksgiving Day.

One additional, over-due change is on its way. We now have a system, which has been tested in several USDA Service Centers, where your name and address and related information will only have to be given once. We will share it among all the USDA Service Center partner agencies. We are committed to making the changes you asked for. We want these changes to be operational, in USDA Service Centers, this year.

I am grateful that most of our employees you deal with each day are thoughtful, knowledgeable and just plain "good neighbors" to you. But until all of us at USDA meet this same ideal of service, we are going to work at improving ourselves.

Again, thank you for helping the USDA do a better job of serving the American people.

—Maureen Kennedy
Chairperson

Top-Line Report

The top-line report seeks to convey the critical points in the most economical manner. It is a combination of bullets and narrative points that are prepared quickly for sharing with the client. These brief reports are prepared primarily from field notes and moderator memory and are presented back to the client within a day or two of the focus group. These reports are also called "top-of-mind reports," a term which is actually more descriptive of the process. Top-line reports are oriented toward the particular decision or problem that gave rise to the focus group. As a result, this report won't contain information unless it is specifically relevant to the purpose of the study. The top-line report is usually an interim or preliminary report that is prepared quickly and provides immediate findings that are expanded on in the later narrative report (sometimes called the full report). Top-line reports vary in length but are usually several pages long.

The top-line report is sometimes confused with the executive summary because they are approximately the same length. The executive summary is derived from the narrative report analysis, is prepared at the conclusion of the narrative report, and seeks to highlight critical points. By contrast, the top-line report is prepared quickly, without benefit of the careful analysis found in the narrative report. The emphasis of top-line reports is speed in reporting.

Top-line reports are standard in market research because sponsors want immediate results. Sponsors often view the groups from behind the one-way mirror and will make decisions based on their own impressions if the analyst doesn't quickly provide a report. In many cases in market research, the study is completed by a seasoned moderator and is very focused (e.g., which ad has greatest appeal), which makes top-line reports straightforward. The top-line report possesses risks for novice moderators and in complex studies. Because they are prepared quickly and with minimal time for reflection, there is danger of error. The first impressions of the sponsor are difficult to modify, and sometimes the rapidly produced top-line report presents concepts that are later discounted, revised, or eliminated completely. The top-line report exists for a particular function—that of providing rapid, yet often sketchy, results to concerned clients.

Top-Line Reports Are Preliminary and May Be Subject to Later Revision

A friend told me about leaving his new car at the airport parking lot. The car was about a week old and his pride and joy. When he returned from the trip, he was shocked to find that the passenger door had a gigantic dent. It was consoling to discover that there was a note under the windshield wiper. His first impression was that the problem was now solved. The handwritten note said, "I banged into your car. There are lots of people watching me. They think I'm writing down my license number, but I'm not."

First Impressions Can Be Wrong

REACHING VULNERABLE YOUTH: KEYS TO SUCCESS

What makes a successful program in working with young people at risk? What are the characteristics of a successful youth worker?

Top-Line Report

Characteristics of Successful Programs

- *Focused and articulated vision*

   Best programs have a clear mission and a vision of how the organization will accomplish the mission.

- *Sustained and holistic approach*

   Best youth programs make long-term commitments to people and integrate needs and strengths of child, family, school, and community.

- *Supportive, flexible atmosphere for staff*

   Best youth programs have rules, policies, and expectations that are flexible and allow for creative problem-solving by staff.

- *Community-based collaboration*

   Best youth programs are created from the community, not from the outside.

COMMENT: While focus group participants often distinguished between the characteristics of people and programs, one cannot exist without the other. Caring, non-judgmental, creative staff cannot function as good youth workers without the support of an effective organization. Likewise, no organization can be effective without qualified people involved.

Bulleted Report

The bulleted report is like an outline of the narrative report, but with carefully chosen phrases and words to convey the concepts clearly. The bulleted report is increasingly gaining popularity because of the speed with which it can be prepared and consumed.

EXAMPLE

Bulleted Report

REDUCING ALCOHOL, TOBACCO, AND
OTHER DRUG PROBLEMS IN THE COMMUNITY

Most Serious Problem
- *Teens' opinion: Internal family conflict*
- *Parents' opinion: Alcohol use by teens*

Attitudes about Alcohol
- *Occasional use by older teens is acceptable*
- *Excessive use or drinking and driving are unacceptable*

Most Effective Preventive Strategy
- *Positive example of parents*
- *Realistic messages are effective*
- *Rules are important*
- *Keep teens busy*

Teen Advice to Parents
- *Listen carefully and offer practical advice*
- *Avoid nagging or lectures*

Influential Adults
- *Show respect, fairness, and consistency in enforcing rules*
- *Provide positive role models through their own behavior*

Suggestions
- *Parents should spend more time with teens*
- *Improve communication skills*
- *Teens can teach parents to communicate*
- *Inventory chemical-free activities for teens*
- *Community groups should work together*
- *Create jobs and community service opportunities*
- *Use cross-age and peer teaching*
- *Extend DARE through middle school*

12

Oral Reports

Overview

A key challenge to oral reporting is to know what type of report you are presenting and then to present your information in the most effective manner. Here are some thoughts about categories of reports and tips that make those reports successful.

Types of Oral Reports—A Continuum of Possibilities

It's a mistake to assume that all oral reports are alike, any more than all written reports are alike. Again, the maxim is that the report, be it written or oral, should be tailored to the circumstances. In some places, the oral report is the primary means of communication, and the written document, if it even exists, serves merely as a reference. Another organization might have an entirely different tradition where the oral report is a mere formality and decisions are based on the written document. Therefore, the guiding principle is to find out the sponsor's traditions and expectations, and to adjust the oral and written reports accordingly.

Oral reports can range from conversational sharing of ideas and findings to formal briefings. You may wish to include more than one of the following types of presentations.

Unstructured Conversational Report

The unstructured conversational report is an informal sharing of results between a team member, volunteer, or focus group participant and another person. These are spontaneous conversations that are not anticipated. Suppose that it's the day after a focus group on organizational morale, and you're walking down the hall on your way to a meeting. The agency head who requested that you to do the focus group study sees you and asks, "Well, how's it going? Learned anything about morale?" This is an opportune moment! You can say that you're not yet ready to share results, or you can use the moment to bring up an early point. Admittedly, it's difficult when the study is not yet complete, and it's virtually impossible unless you've given it some thought. Yet, this teachable moment might not happen again.

This is perhaps the most neglected form of oral reporting. Unfortunately, too often the researcher does not anticipate the opportunity to share and is caught unaware. As a result, the messages presented are typically immediate unthinking reactions, highlighting the unusual results or emphasizing trivia. In the worst form, the messages can be harmful to the study because they confuse the recipient. Often, the results are given in the form of a story—perhaps an example shared by a focus group participant. Researchers should anticipate these opportunities and encourage team members to reflect on what they might say. Indeed, the team members might actually practice with each other and offer feedback and suggestions to others on the team to ensure consistency, clarity, and accuracy.

Structured Conversational Report

The structured conversational report is similar to the unstructured conversational report, except that the contents of the report are planned in advance and organized in a systematic manner. This reporting consists of one-to-one sharing of results, sometimes with a short handout of bulleted findings, a top-line report, or an executive summary. If more time is available, a complete narrative report could also be given. Sometimes, researchers have considerable time to organize their thoughts and structure the report, but in other situations, such as sponsor debriefings, the timing can be almost immediate. What is distinctive about the structured conversational report is that the content is deliberately arranged, but interruptions or questions can occur throughout the conversation. Therefore, the reporter must be thoroughly familiar with the information and able to adjust emphasis or points, depending on the conversation.

Sponsor Debriefing

In the market research tradition, the moderator concludes the focus group and then goes behind the one-way mirror to conduct a debriefing with the sponsor. The moderator or analyst has literally seconds to arrange the findings. Those who are most successful at this task anticipate the report from the moment they begin the focus group. Analysis and sharing results are thought about throughout the discussion, and, after a bit of experience, the results can be impressive. The debriefing usually addresses only the focus group that the sponsors observed, although the analyst might compare and contrast the discussion with those held previously.

Informal Briefing

The informal briefing is a short presentation to a committee or business meeting. Handouts are often used. This report is unique because it addresses the series of focus groups and presents findings in an informal manner. Points are carefully organized for brevity and completeness. In some situations, participants interrupt, challenge, ask questions, or reinforce the points. Other times, there are no interruptions, and questions are asked at the end of the presentation. Those who are most successful at informal briefings are clear about the major points and keep coming back to reinforce those central themes.

Formal Briefing

The formal briefing is orderly, civilized, and guided by traditions and rules. As a result, it tends to be more organized and involves the recipient to a lesser extent. There are fewer interruptions, and the reporter is given a time allotment that he or she is expected to fill. Following the presentation, participants are expected to ask questions. Handouts can be used effectively in this kind of format.

Formal Presentation/Lecture/Professional Meeting

At the highest level of structure, the formal presentation is often used for larger groups where exact amounts of time are allocated and questions may challenge the methodology, the findings, or the recommendations. Again, handouts should be used, and visuals are often desirable. These presentations are typical at annual meetings and professional societies.

Tips on Oral Reporting

Here are some suggestions that we would like to pass on about oral reporting. Experts tend to use these strategies, and indeed, we developed them from observing the best oral reports.

Allow Time for Questions

Before preparing the oral briefing or presentation, the speaker should find out how much time is available, where the report will be given, and who the audience will be. Those receiving an oral report usually wish to discuss findings, respond to the results, or ask questions. The most successful oral reports often allocate only one third to one half of the time for the presentation; the remainder is spent in follow-up discussion. Therefore, a 15-minute report may include a 5-minute presentation and 10 minutes for questions, clarifications, and discussion of future action.

Sequence Your Comments

The first few minutes in an oral report are critical because the speaker needs to set the stage quickly for the presentation of findings. The speaker should carefully lay out the framework, describing why the study is important to the audience. The oral presentation must focus on the key points, citing the most important finding first and then moving to less important findings. Within these first few moments, the speaker should high-light several key factors. For example: Why was the study needed? What do we know now that we didn't know before? How can these finding be used? It is important to engage the audience quickly, to involve them in the report, to hook them into the study, and to explain clearly why the research effort was important.

The outline used in the written report does not transfer well to oral reporting. Often, researchers assume that a report is a report, whether it be oral or written, and that the sequence of information presented should be consistent in both kinds of reports. Oral reporting is different, and it requires special fore-thought and preparation. Some communications experts have recommended that the most important points be presented at the end of an oral presentation—that lesser points build toward the most critical point. This recommendation does not work well in evaluation or research reporting. Most reporting occurs in envi-ronments where people have time restrictions and limited pa-tience, and where interruptions regularly occur. In these situ-ations, brevity and conciseness are valued. Thus, the most important findings are better placed at the top of the list.

Be Careful of the Ho-Hum Syndrome

When planning for the oral report, it is helpful to consider the ho-hum syndrome, a predictable reaction of many decision makers. Ho-hum is best characterized by the questions going through the minds of the audience, such as: Do we really need this study? Don't we know this already? We paid to have some-body study this? Shouldn't this staff member be doing something really important instead of conducting these studies? To us, the results may seem enormously important with far-reaching impli-cations, but to a busy decision maker, they can sound like hair-splitting and avoidance of real work. Much of what we discover in program evaluation and research efforts does tend to sound like common sense, and this tendency needs to be defused in the oral presentation. Often, the best procedure is to address it head-on by saying, "This study is of importance because. . . ." You can also tell the audience what the other possible hypotheses were, that we now know the correct course of action, and, as a result, time and resources are saved.

Limit Your Points

Attempt to present oral reports with fewer than seven points. This recommendation stems from studies in cognitive psychology that suggest that short-term memory capacity for most people is limited to five to seven items. In addition, use short, active phrases to describe points as opposed to complete sentences. These brief phrases are designed to do two things: to convey the important concepts and to be easily remembered.

Use Visuals and Quotes

Visuals can effectively highlight the points. Key points and quotes tend to be more memorable when displayed visually. Selected quotations or even brief tape recordings of actual comments can also be very effective in the oral report, but they must be used in moderation. When it comes to visuals, the researcher has an array of options at differing levels of technology. One of the most basic is the briefing chart. This can be made on poster-board or foamboard and used to highlight key points. In addition, these charts can be reproduced as smaller 8½-by-11-inch hand-outs and shared with the audience. Investigate the possibility of using presentation software on your computer. Professional-quality results can be obtained with minimal skill. Equipment is available to project computer results on the screen, and portable large screen displays are just around the corner.

Tell Your Audience What You Want Them to Do

Sometimes, the purpose of the oral report is unclear to the audience. We have observed the presentation of oral reports to organizations, and when the reporter was finished, the group members just looked at each other for a few awkward moments. This uncomfortable silence was then followed by the type of action typical of elected bodies. Someone usually moved that the report be approved or accepted so they could then move on to really important matters. In these situations, the group receiving the oral report did not know why they were receiving the briefing because they were never told why it was being presented. At the beginning or end of the report, the reporter should have indicated what action was recommended or why the report was presented, such as to provide a briefing, to form a study committee, to continue discussion at a later time, to seek funds to implement the findings, to approve a new course of action, and so on. It is dangerous to assume that the audience will know what to do with the report.

Select the Right Reporter

Some people have a natural or acquired talent for preparing written reports or presenting oral reports. Select your reporter based on ability and credibility, not because of his or her role in the focus group interview. Some individuals are gifted in presenting findings, and these people should be considered when selecting the reporter. As important, however, is the credibility of the reporter. At times, a volunteer or someone from outside of the agency or organization is deemed more credible. The best choice is to have an individual who is both skillful and credible present the results.

Naturally, the reporter will need to be sufficiently acquainted with both the process and findings. The reporter should practice the oral report and allow sufficient time for preparation and collegial feedback. Hastily prepared reports often have awkward construction, vague points, misspellings, and other problems that limit their acceptance by users.

Postscript:
For Graduate Students Only

Graduate students regularly ask about the possibility of using focus groups as research in graduate dissertations: "Can I actually use focus groups in my study?" We'd like to reflect on their concerns.

The dissertation is a quest for knowledge and an opportunity to discover insights into theories and concepts. This is a lofty goal and an important perspective. The purpose of the dissertation, from a faculty view, is for the student to demonstrate expertise in research, to show mastery of a field of study, to undertake independent study, and to do all these things at a level of excellence typical of the institution. The examination committee exists for the purpose of evaluating the quality of the product.

It is critical for you, the student, to know the basis on which you will be judged. Typically, it will be on the manner and procedures used in conducting the research. While it may be satisfying to you to make discoveries that are beneficial and have theoretical or practical benefits, these alone will not constitute a successful defense of your dissertation. The test is the degree to which you followed prescribed rules. If modifications were made, you must understand and be able to explain the theoretical basis and consequences of those changes.

Therefore, it is essential that you be well grounded in whatever research procedure used. You are expected to perform the research procedure according to accepted specifications. Your ability to do this is acquired from training, study, and experience.

Before we go further, let's address the opening question in two parts. First, can focus groups in general be used as a research procedure in graduate dissertations? The second question is more specific and must be answered by you, in concurrence with your adviser. The question is, should focus groups be used as the research procedure in your study?

The answer to the first question is clear. Yes, focus group research can be used in graduate dissertations. Focus groups can be used alone or with other research procedures. The answer to the second question is, it depends. Here are some topics that you may wish to consider as you reflect on your specific study.

1. What's the case for focus groups in this particular study?

Do focus groups fit your research specifications? How do focus groups compare with alternative means of gathering information? What specifically makes focus group research appropriate for your study? What is the case against using focus groups? Every research procedure has disadvantages and limitations. Know how you will respond to these questions. Remember that research begins with the problem or question; the methodology flows out of that problem or question.

2. What's the tradition of your department or university?

Graduate universities, and degree programs within those institutions, can vary greatly in what they consider to be acceptable research procedures. Some are extraordinarily bound by tradition, while others are open to emerging research procedures. Find out what the range has been in the past. Does the climate foster differing research paradigms? Look over dissertations completed in the past few years, and categorize the research procedures. What variation has taken place? You are at greater risk when you use a research procedure unfamiliar to faculty. When faculty do not understand or accept the epistemology of a particular research procedure, they will likely have difficulty in evaluating the dissertation. Focus group research is relatively new in academic research. Don't be surprised if you find that it hasn't been done in your department.

Suppose that you find no studies using focus group interviewing. Does that mean that you can't do it? Not necessarily. Quite a number of faculty are open and eager to examine and use emerging research procedures. In fact, some faculty may see the chance to work with you as a co-learning opportunity to discover more about a topic of interest. If this occurs, your role will change slightly, and you will be seen as the leader of the discovery team. In this role, you will be expected to understand the research procedures thoroughly, to stay in regular communication with faculty, and to keep them abreast of concerns, issues, and developments.

3. Do you have time and access to resources?

Qualitative research often takes more time to collect and analyze data than does quantitative research. Focus group research for a dissertation can be a substantial time investment, and it may also require money for food, travel, facilities, or honorariums. You'll need to tape record and, if at all possible, to type the transcripts yourself. You'll be expected to know your data thoroughly. Usually, you will also want to use a computer analysis program to document that your procedures are systematic and verifiable. Before you get too far into the planning, consider the resources needed for success. Can you make the time investment? Do you have resources available? If you don't have the resources, can you get them from somewhere else?

4. Do you have the skills?

Do you have the necessary skills to conduct focus group research? You may need to seek training, locate a mentor, and develop your personal experience. The dissertation should not be your first experience with conducting focus groups. Volunteer your time and conduct some focus groups for an organization before you use them for your graduate study.

5. Is your adviser supportive?

Early on, discuss the possibility of focus group research with your adviser. You absolutely must have the support and confidence of the person directing your thesis or dissertation. Don't proceed unless your adviser approves.

6. Do you have the right committee members?

Select your committee carefully. Find people who understand qualitative research, have had experience with it, and are flexible and open to inquiry. Incidentally, don't assume that, just because they are knowledgeable or experienced with qualitative research, they are open to differing research procedures, including focus groups. Be sure that your committee is accepting of focus groups in the way that you wish to use them. Stay in touch with your committee.

7. Do you have a sound and defensible design?

Plan the study carefully. Have enough focus groups. Be certain that you are listening to the right people. Consider the benefits of multiple methods, including quantitative as well as qualitative research.

8. Can you meet the expectations of human subjects committees?

More Information on Consent Forms is Included in *Planning Focus Groups*

In most universities, the student must meet the requirements of human subjects committees which document that participants are adequately informed of the study and are participating willingly. Often, the focus group participants must read and sign a statement acknowledging that they are willing participants. The challenge to you is to prepare the consent form so that it conveys appropriate information without unduly providing background information that could sway or limit the sharing. As you seek to meet this human subjects requirement, remember the unique characteristics that make a focus group work. Part of the challenge is to provide sufficient advance information so that participants are aware of the study but not so much information that participants rush to solutions before they fully articulate and understand the problem. Unless this statement is prepared carefully, it can constrain and limit the thought process of participants. Moreover, be careful to maintain the permissive, informal, and nonthreatening atmosphere that is essential to the focus group. Legal-sounding documents that need signatures can work against you.

9. Can you verify results with participants when you are finished?

Share the findings and conclusions with participants and invite their comments. After all groups are completed and you have prepared your findings, you may seek to verify these results with the participants. This could be in writing or, preferably, in person. This process of verification serves several purposes. At the most basic level, it seeks to present findings back to participants as a check to ensure that the findings are correct. You can also use this opportunity to present your interpretation and to encourage and entertain other interpretations. In addition, you can open a discussion of implications and recommendations. Another purpose of the verification process is unique to the public sector and represents a philosophy of research that you may wish to adopt. The philosophy is that researchers who ask the community for help in obtaining information should give back to that community as much as, or more than, what they received. Admittedly, not all researchers share this view, but give thought to how sharing results fits your philosophy and applies to your study.

10. Do you have the self-discipline?

This project is going to take lots of work, and you will regularly need to discipline yourself to continue—like after a long day at work, or when your family wants attention, or when you can think of a thousand more enjoyable things to do. Qualitative research tends to be ill-structured, and you will feel that you are continually making difficult decisions. Sometimes, students are drawn to qualitative research because they have difficulties with quantitative research. They consider statistics to be too difficult, and focus groups seem so easy when compared with quantitative procedures. Think again! Focus groups, like other forms of qualitative research, will demand superb skills in listening, analyzing, and writing. Many faculty consider statistical procedures to be easier and faster for dissertation research. Qualitative research is not the easy path!

A department chair at a large university called in the graduate faculty and offered advice on graduate student research design. He suggested that the faculty be more discerning about which students are encouraged to conduct qualitative research. He told the faculty, "Our university, like many others, has students with a range of talents. Some are of extraordinary talent, and others just get by. We're having difficulty getting our marginal students to defend their dissertations successfully. I recommend that we encourage our marginal students to do quantitative studies, because the research protocols are well structured, we can continuously monitor their progress, and it requires less judgment."

BACKGROUND

Let the Marginal Students Do Quantitative Studies

References

Beveridge, W. I. B. (1957). *The art of scientific investigation.* New York: Vintage.

Collier, T. (1996, October). *The secret life of moderators.* Paper presented at the meeting of the Qualitative Research Consultants Association, Montreal, Canada. (Available from Trevor Collier & Co. Ltd., Qualitative Research Consultants, 88 Leuty Ave., Toronto, Ontario, M4E 2R4, Canada)

George, W. H. (1936). *The scientist in action. A scientific study of his methods.* London: Williams & Norgate Ltd. Quoted in W. I. B. Beveridge. (1957). *The art of scientific investigation.* New York: Vintage.

Glaser, B., & Strauss, A. (1967). *The discovery of grounded theory.* Chicago: Aldine.

Guba, E. G., & Lincoln, Y. S. (1989). *Fourth generation evaluation.* Newbury Park, CA: Sage.

LeBoeuf, M. (1985). *Getting results!* New York: Berkley Books.

Miles, M. B., & Weitzman, E. A. (1994). Choosing computer programs for qualitative data analysis. Appendix in M. B. Miles & A. M. Huberman, *Qualitative data analysis.* Thousand Oaks, CA: Sage.

Patton, M. Q. (1990). *Qualitative evaluation and research methods.* Thousand Oaks, CA: Sage.

Richards, T., & Richards, L. (1994). Using computers in qualitative analysis. In N. Denzin & Y. Lincoln, eds., *Handbook of qualitative research.* Thousand Oaks, CA: Sage.

Strauss, A. L., & Corbin, J. (1990). *Basics of qualitative research: Grounded theory procedures and techniques.* Thousand Oaks, CA: Sage.

Tesch, R. (1990). *Qualitative research: Analysis types and software tools.* New York: Falmer.

Weitzman, E., & Miles, M. B. (1994). *Computer programs for qualitative data analysis.* Thousand Oaks, CA: Sage.

Index to This Volume

Index to the Focus Group Kit

The letter preceding the page number refers to the volume, according to the following key:

About the Author

Richard A. Krueger is a professor and evaluation leader at the University of Minnesota. He teaches in the College of Education and Human Development and serves as an evaluation specialist with the University of Minnesota Extension Service. Over the past decade, he has taught hundreds of people to plan, conduct, and analyze focus group interviews. He loves stories. Perhaps that is what drew him to focus group interviews. Where else can one hear so many stories in such a short period of time?